THE LAND OF WAR ELEPHANTS

Travels Beyond the Pale

Afghanistan, Pakistan, and India

Mathew Wilson

Nomad Press
A division of Nomad Communications
10 9 8 7 6 5 4 3 2 1
Copyright © 2003 Mathew J. A. Wilson

All photographs are by Mathew Wilson unless otherwise credited. The photographs of
the Gardner china and the Lashkargargh/Qala Bist artifacts were taken by Images
Plus/Charles A. Parker.

ISBN 0-9659258-9-7

Questions regarding the ordering of this book should be addressed to
Independent Publishers Group
814 N. Franklin St.
Chicago, IL 60610

Nomad Press, PO Box 875, Norwich, VT 05055
www.nomadpress.net

Front Cover Photo:
Fatehpur Sikri. The Victory Gate. Mathew Wilson.

Back Cover Photo:
A Young Prince. Photograph by Lala Din Dayal. Deccan, Hyderbad c1890. Identity of the
subject unknown. Private Collection. By permission of The Metropolitan Museum of Art.

Acknowledgements

My list of thanks runs deeper than routine acknowledgement. At the start I thank Alex and Susan Kahan of Nomad Press for their enthusiasm and support for a book that was very much in its formative stage when they first saw it, and Susan particularly for her final incisive editing. My editors were my salvation. Anna Typrowicz, who first read and commented on the text, suffered the worst of an overweight draft and my sometimes less-than-brilliant synthesis of two styles of English. Lauri Berkenkamp, who played the major part, not only held my hand whenever I wandered, but was a guardian and guiding spirit. The darkest days, when ongoing events in Afghanistan, Pakistan, and India in 2002 came close to throwing me off course, turned to the light of calm purpose whenever I saw her. The format of the book, the design and text, the maps, the chapter heads, and the fine-tuning of the covers, all of which realize the book I first envisaged, is the work of Bruce Leasure. The Nomad Press team was vital to me, and, beyond the bonding production of a book, are friends.

There is no way in which I can adequately thank Janet for sharing the greater part of these journeys with me. As I look back at our earlier travels, and re-read my journals and notes, I cannot conceive how I could have expected her to share such ventures, let alone with a two-year old, and well advanced in her second pregnancy. More often than not our living conditions rated low on any scale; and the outcome, both at the setting out, and on any given day, was often far from certain. When, right at the very start, we arrived in Quetta, it seemed we'd never survive our first winter in our unheated house. Come mid-winter, when the the 100-degree heat of summer was still unimaginable, I wrote her a little poem to thank her for staying the course. It was doggerel, no more than that; but perhaps it will serve here as a more public declaration of my appreciation, admiration, and love:

> I took my wife to Quetta where the peaches grow
> and the clear mountain air is like a long cool drink.
> I went there myself, and because I had to go,
> she came because she loved me, or so I like to think.

But there the earth was hard and the rivers were stone,
the drains were filled with ice, and the mountains snow white,
and the Kandahar wind made tough Baluchis moan
as they huddled round their squat Quetta stoves all night.

I took my wife to Quetta where the peaches grow
And found the grip of winter made it seem as though
I'd taken her to Lhasa, or to the tundra's brink;
but she came because she loved me, or so I like to think.

Quetta, Baluchistan. February 1968.

Quetta, measured against some of our later travels in the region, could be classed as a minor paradise.

For Victoria Mary Wilson Roskill

Born 31 August 1968
at the Combined Military Hospital
Quetta, Baluchistan

I write of her place of birth
and
of places where we have traveled together

Contents

Introduction

An innate English reticence, a reluctance to talk about oneself or close family, slows my hand as I write, but an introduction is needed. Voluntarily or involuntarily, my family have played a part in the chapters that follow. Janet, my wife. Edward, our son. Victoria, our daughter. Janet and I now live in Vermont, having moved from England, eighteen years ago. Edward also crossed the Atlantic, and now lives in Concord, Massachusetts. Only our daughter, Victoria, remains in England, living and working in London. She was due to have her first child in late November 2001. Her pregnancy had been complicated by toxoplasmosis. Janet and I had decided to fly to London to hold her hand for two weeks in September, in addition to returning later for the childbirth, and staying on, through Christmas.

It happened that our scheduled flight date to London proved to be the catalyst that prompted my attention to the completion of this book, which was already in the making. I start with 9/11, but this book is not targeted on this, nor subsequent events. It is a book of travels, a story telling. It goes back into the past, and ends, but dwells briefly, in October 2002, the time I finished writing.

Boston. 11 September 2001

With a 9:00 am departure time, we'd taken a hotel courtesy bus to Boston's Logan Airport at around six in the morning. Our only companions on that ride were the crew of an American Airlines flight bound for San Francisco, with a departure time close to ours. We too were flying American, with London, England, as our destination. The link was close enough to set a bond. In the early sunlight of a clear day we joked, teased each other, and laughed as we headed down the McClelland Highway from the Logan Holiday Inn, where we'd all staged overnight.

At our departure gate we found AA156 shared a departure area with their flight, but our new friends had long since boarded their aircraft. We settled down for the hour or more we'd have to wait before we were called forward. It was hard to guess which of the captive passengers were San Francisco bound and which were London bound. Time passed. Waiting periods in departure lounges, somehow, rarely seem interminable. What do you do? What do we all do? Read the morning papers, drink coffee, talk to people, and watch people . . . The San Francisco flight was called. We thinned out by some fifty percent. We now knew who our fellow passengers were to be for the next six hours.

What triggers primitive subliminal instinct? One man had caught my attention. I'd long singled him out, even in the crowd scene, as highly unlikely ever to make my temporary friendship list. "Pity we still have him with us," I remarked, sotto voce, to Janet. "Let's hope he's seated nowhere near us." The San Francisco flight pulled away from the ramp.

The subject of my indefinable aversion had never taken a seat in the departure lounge, and now, even with a full aircraft load of empty seats open for choice, remained on his feet, in motion like a caged animal. There was a tangible nervousness, a near-feral agitation there, and in his pacing he never relaxed his grip on a small roll-on with an attached brief-case. The whole time he held a cellphone glued to his right ear, but he appeared to be on receive only. I never saw him speak into it. Was he American? Maybe, given the national ethnic mix, but he certainly seemed alien to New England. A dark complexion. Tinted glasses. Leather, or a look-like it jacket. The cut was not American. European? German? His height? About five feet, ten inches. Age? Late twenties, early thirties. At the gate mothers with young and some first and business class passengers, anticipating a call forward, were already assembling. I saw him push forward, rudely, to the start line. "Look at that jerk" I said to Janet."We've all got boarding passes. Does he think someone's going to take his seat?"

Boarding started. We ditched our newspapers. When I next looked at the gate area, he'd gone. When we boarded he was sitting in an aisle seat in first class, in the row closest to the cockpit door. A glass of amber-colored liquid on ice was already in his hand. Whiskey at nine in the morning? It wasn't only the hour that surprised me, but the apparent error of my subliminal assessment of his probable faith.

The captain announced our flight time to London. Takeoff checks completed, we were on the runway, ready to roll. The brakes were released, the sound of the engines changed, and then power went instantly to idle. A second announcement: "I don't know why, but we've been ordered by the tower to return to the gate. They won't give me a reason." On our way back the captain had a third message. "I've just been told that when we get to the gate, the door will be opened. You are to leave the aircraft immediately with all your belongings and wait in the departure lounge. I can't tell you more than this."

The airline staff at the gate were ashen, some were in tears. Other passengers were already at the gate, and within minutes the departure area became a shoulder-to-shoulder mass of bewildered people, pressed closer and closer together as those near the ceiling-mounted TV monitors, fixated on the screens, would not move. I caught one glimpse of our first class passenger forcing his way towards the concourse. The tidal pressure of still-disembarking passengers washed us just near enough to a TV screen in time to see the first video shot of the San Francisco flight hitting the World Trade Center. State troopers arrived, spread out, and shouted orders to evacuate the terminal using every security gate.

Later, much later, called forward flight by flight, we collected our checked bags. There was no sign of that one passenger.

Working our way around Revere and North Boston to avoid a city gridlocked by the evacuation of every high-rise building, we were forced by traffic further and further to the northeast. We abandoned trying to seek refuge with Edward and Imogen in Concord. Our car radio had been on since we left the airport, and the magnitude of events that morning hit like successive hammer blows. Imo, contacted by cellphone, was vital. Eventually, for the trans-Atlantic circuits were virtually jammed, she reached Victoria, who had no news of American Airlines Flight 156. Later we too got a call through to her as we drove on, back to Vermont. At this point you might ask did I contact anyone to report my suspicions? The answer is yes, I did. Was he alone? That I couldn't say. My attention had been centered on the one man.

Nine-Eleven brought Afghanistan, Pakistan, and India to the front of the world stage for the rest of that year and through 2002. For our family, none of these countries was unknown territory. Janet and I lived in Pakistan for a year in 1968, and our daughter Victoria was born there. We had traveled twice in Afghanistan, and I returned there a third time. We returned to Pakistan in 1984. We travelled in India that year too, and later, in 1989–90, and 1996. In those first weeks as Afghanistan was turned into an Armageddon, I opened long-stored files to find my maps, and re-read my journals and notes. That day at Logan, and the months that followed, were the catalyst that prompted this book, which I started sketching out while Janet and I were in London in November and December of 2001. The child, a boy, was born without complication, and both his mother, and he, who have visited us three times in the United States already, seem radiant, happy, and healthy.

Vermont. 2002–2003

I write of travel, and I write of a time when travel was different. Of a time before the world had progressed to the hijacking of passenger aircraft to be used as suicidal missiles of mass devastation. Of a time when it was possible to venture into remote areas, the threat of banditry always accepted. Of a time when a travel agent rarely had a hand in your travel arrangements. You were much on your own. Of a time when learning and understanding the form, shape, and feel of physical geography, and the casual, accidental, happenstance contact with the peoples whose land you were crossing was your motivation. Sometimes the risks in getting there, and being there, were marginally higher than one might wish, but in many cases it was often sad to realize that it was time to head back, to return home.

My broad canvas is Central Asia, and South Asia in particular. Three countries, which, linked historically, have long shared little in common save that linkage. The geographic title is too bland, too generic for an area better known anciently for its inclination to repel rather than welcome its neighbors, let alone alien visitors. Right at the start of recorded history it was described as the land of the war elephants. I see no reason to change that title today. I write first of mountain country, the land we know as Afghanistan, and in part, Pakistan. High ground has a compulsive magnetism. For thousands of years distant mountains have drawn men to seek what might be found in their hidden valleys and whatever might lie on the far side of the range, if indeed the mountains could be crossed. The jagged complexity and altitude of some of these massive walls form barriers that are close to absolute. They have shaped, and are still shaping, the course of history. The central Asian divide, the Hindu Kush, Pamirs, Karakorams, and the multi-named mass of the Himalayas are the greatest of these ranges.

Here, in the ice caverns of the high altitudes, are the sources of the great rivers of civilization, the Indus, Ganges, Mekong, Yangtze, and the Yellow River. Many other rivers have had a significant effect on events, not the least of them the Oxus, or Amu Darya as we call it now. Its course, running to the north and parallel to the Hindu Kush, has long set part of Afghanistan's northern limits. The territory on the far bank was the Soviet Union then. It is Tajikistan and Uzbekistan now. This river and this region were well known to Alexander the Great. Only in late 2001 did it become increasingly familiar to us. If you would travel because you are drawn by geography and history, it is to these places, and to India, long the richest prize in Central Asia, that you would go, or would have gone in times past.

The great rivers of India have served as the arteries of civilization, with the Ganges the aorta of northern India. The Grand Trunk Road, which ran from the Khyber Pass to the heartland of India, went this way, first crossing the five rivers of the Punjab, to reach Lahore. All of this is in Pakistan now. From the border near Amritsar the great road continued on to Delhi, to Varanasi, the place we once called Benares, to end in Calcutta, favoring the banks of the Ganges for much of this distance. My travels followed this ancient route. Much of my interest was driven by history, research for lectures, notes for a book, and much of my story line lay that way. However, the coastal cities also featured in my travels: and I write here of Karachi, Mumbai (Bombay), and Goa. It was in these landing places, the one-time river mouth fishing villages, that we, the alien European nations, first sought enrichment through trade, then territory, and then, ultimately, sought to implant our religion, laws, language, and lifestyle on a subcontinent.

Your ability to roam in Afghanistan, Pakistan, and India, as we did, no longer exists in a world that is now generating proscriptions and hatreds, and building new barriers, most as absolute as the walls, razor wire, and minefields of the Iron Curtain. You may conclude that something has gone wrong, internationally, somewhere along the line since that dreadful wall was leveled in Berlin. As I look at Central Asia and see its countries taken as chess pieces, sublimated into being no more than the agents, or opponents, of grand strategy, I feel less than easy. But my primary purpose is not to comment on the exercise of world power. It is simply to record some of our travels in the region, and some of my side trips, for Janet was not always with me. It is story telling, but in it you may find threads that have a bearing on events today.

Despite this last caveat, my prelude may have made what is to follow sound grand, and perhaps academic. It is not. I write principally of people and places, of travel, and all that I have said here simply defines the lie of the land.

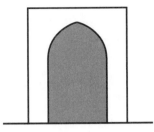

Afghanistan

One

Between the Indus and the Oxus

 It was 1967. I was a thirty-three-year-old Light Infantry Captain in the British Army, at that time stationed in England. Janet, twenty-four, was the veteran of a marriage that had already taken her to Malaya for two years. Our son Edward was one. At my age and rank I faced a career hurdle. In most armies a staff college qualification is a near vital endorsement if you're to stay on the corporate escalator. Having already seen active service in Cyprus, Borneo, and Aden, I found the prospect less than attractive. You didn't need a crystal ball to see it all: endless study for the entry examinations, a year at a staff college, and the certainty that most of your future career would then be spent tied to a desk, exactly what I'd joined the army to avoid. I took the entrance examination as a gamble, not unduly concerned about the result, and somehow my name came up on the 1968 list of those selected for entry.

Thank heaven there were choices to be made. Attend your own staff college at Camberley, or opt for one of a short list of reciprocal colleges abroad? Australia, India, New Zealand, Pakistan, or the USA? Each offered just two vacancies a year. Word had it that not attending Camberley was professional suicide. You needed to learn the cries of the day, the politically correct way of going about your business; make friends in your peer group; and hopefully find a patron in the hierarchy above your rank. My decision making was subliminal. Five generations of my forebears had worn regimental uniform at some time in their lives. Two had served in India, one at the time of the Great Mutiny of 1857–58 and the other, my grandfather, at the zenith of the British Raj, a climax marked by the Delhi Coronation Durbar in 1911. The British Indian Army Staff College had been established in Quetta, Baluchistan, which was now a part of Pakistan; at independence the College had rolled itself into the Pakistan Army Command and Staff College. I chose Quetta.

The choice carried with it two rather daunting results. The first was learning that you were given an unlimited baggage allowance, and expected to take all your clothing, food, and necessities for one year. Virtually nothing could be bought in Quetta. The second was that the anticipated mountain of supplies, to say nothing of a car, could never be transported by air. Travel to Pakistan was by sea, with the shortest direct line, a Lloyd Triestino weekly passenger-freight service from Venice, through the Suez Canal to Karachi. With Tim and Gilly Eastwood, the other British pair, plus Seymour (two and a half) and Henry (eight months), we were booked to travel that way.

In the largest government departments the light of day takes time to penetrate. The Ministry of Defence clearly was no exception. Unfortunately, sunken ships had blocked the Suez Canal since the Arab-Israeli Six-Day War, earlier that year. Lloyd Triestino had changed its schedule. Our first-class tickets for the *Asia*, sailing from Venice for Karachi on 4 January 1968, were entirely valid, but the one week direct run through the Red Sea was already history, and the *Asia* was following a cruise ship itinerary. Our ports of call were Brindisi, Barcelona, Las Palmas, Capetown, Mombasa (with two days ashore for a safari), and Karachi. Clearly attendance at a staff college offered some benefits.

How much toilet paper do you use in a year? How many tubes of toothpaste? What about toothbrushes? Soap? Think of bacon, butter? Baby food? And while you're on the "B"s, your bar. Despite sending much of our freight ahead to the ship, quite apart from our shipboard suitcases we still had thirty-three crates between the two families, sixteen of which were too heavy for one man to carry. A team of Olympic weight lifters, even without three toddlers in tow, might have declined to travel across Europe as we were about to do, for the Army Movements staff had put together a ship-joining Movement Order that a mental dwarf would have rejected. We were to travel to Venice by rail. The London train went no further than Dover. Everything had to be transferred to a Channel ferry. After the crossing we had to take a train from Calais to Paris. There we were to transfer to the Venice-bound Simplon Express in less than half an hour. What would happen in Venice was not addressed. Either fine judgement or pure negligence ensured that the instruction reached us just forty-eight hours before the *Asia* was due to sail.

The Gare du Lyon in Paris was like a crowd scene in hell; it was rush hour, and it was the children's feeding time. We reached Venice the next morning. The *Asia* was due to sail that afternoon. The thirty-three crates were no longer with us. We had nothing but the clothes we stood in and some baby paraphernalia. Tim and I saw Janet and Gilly and the children into their cabins, and stayed in Venice to find our missing baggage. Twenty-four hours later we joined the ship in Brindisi with the missing boxes, having enlisted every railway porter, commandeered every flat-bed cart at the station, and caused urban traffic paralysis as we pushed our train of carts to the docks. The rest was plain sailing. We were lucky. We didn't lose a child overboard, and we survived a typhoon in the Mozambique Channel, during which the *Asia* rolled within two degrees of the limit of her stability.

In Karachi a fair-headed man, unmistakably English in his tropical suit, introduced himself as the British Military Adviser. He'd come down from Rawalpindi to meet us. After an interminable time spent acquiring import permits for our baggage, we drove to the mendaciously named Beach Luxury Hotel. There was snow in Quetta, we were told, and the Bolan Pass was blocked. Tim and I were to make our way there by train, the *Bolan Mail*, in two days time, with the baggage. Janet and Gilly were to stay in Karachi, and follow, by air, as soon as we'd settled into our quarters. Our wives and children were left to digest the plan.

Tim and I were taken into the bathroom. Our greeter turned on the taps and took a seat on the edge of the tub. "Now let me tell you what the form is . . ." We sat like seagulls in a row on the edge of the bath. He spoke of grand politics, of Russia and China, as hot and cold water cascaded into the great Edwardian bathtub. It was unbelievable. It was pure Graham Greene.

If you want to understand this part of Pakistan and Afghanistan, you must first look at a map. You could say the Indus marks the boundary of ancient India. Draw a straight line from Sukkor on the Indus to Kandahar in Afghanistan. The line runs through two mountain passes: the Bolan and the Khojak. The first pass runs through a range of mountains, the Sulaiman Range, up to Baluchistan, a six-thousand-foot plateau. By then the land of the five great rivers you've left behind is another world. Here the terrain, bare rock, hard sand, and mountain, rarely offers water or softens to vegetation. The straight line you ruled continues through another range, the Khojak, and that second pass. Now you're in Afghanistan, with Kandahar just sixty miles away. The land is much the same. It's tough. Forbidding. Quetta (the name comes from kwatta, a fort) lies on that road. It's the mid-point.

There's a second route into Afghanistan to the east, from Peshawar, a short march from the Indus, through the Khyber Pass to Jalalabad. It's the route most people have heard of, but both routes served the successive invaders who plunged down through the mountain passes, sword in hand, to take the spoils of the rich, fertile, northern plains of India. Semiramis, the great warrior queen of Assyria, a thousand years before the birth of Christ, crossed this near-barren, windswept, winter-cold and summer-baked harsh tribal land, and chose the Bolan route. The Khyber, in time, became the preferred route, chosen by Alexander, and the Moghuls in their turn.

Reversing the course, as it were, from Kandahar and Jalalabad both roads led to Kabul, and from Kabul, a single road switch-backed over the Hindu Kush by way of another pass, the Kowtal-e-Salang, down to the river plain of the Amu Darya, the Oxus. You've passed through a part of the greatest mountain chain in the world by then, and at that point you're in another country. Mongolia. These high plateaus guarded by their barrier ranges, this land between the Oxus and the Indus, thin air country between a mile to well over twice that in elevation, was territory I'd long wanted to see. Another reason why I chose Quetta.

This area has long been vital ground for every player in the Asian league, the "stan" states that were once part of Russia and the Soviet Union, Iran, Pakistan, Kashmir, British India, India, and China. Embedded in its heartland is one major (albeit non-volcanic) seismic fault zone. In one name, it's Afghanistan. Even without the Taliban and Osama bin Laden, the area was as stable as a primed grenade with a rusting pin, and at that time, in 1968, on the far side of the Oxus, we faced the Iron Curtain. The Soviet Union.

You could ask, given these apparently perennial conditions, why would the British have sited a Staff College in Quetta? Quite simply because that was where the action was. You could hardly fail to focus on the business in hand. There was also another plus. You were in "safe" tribal land there, in Muslim warrior country, surrounded by people the British reckoned to be infinitely more trustworthy than the Hindus, who, after the shock of the 1857 Mutiny, were considered suspect, and effete.

The *Bolan Mail* is one of the great train journeys of the world. The first part, paralleling the right bank of the Indus to Sukkur, is dull. But shortly after you've passed through Sibi, you are at the foot of the Bolan Pass and the track curves and tunnels as it clings, climbing all the while, through the ravine cut by the Bolan River. The mountains on each side rise to eight thousand and ten thousand feet and it's bitterly cold in February as the harsh Quetta wind scythes down the narrow pass. The halts were deserted. At Hirok the only movement was the streaming wind-torn prayer flags on a tiny crenelated whitewashed mosque. At Kolpur we took water from a tower covered in icicles. The high plateau we reached at Spezand seemed limitless, bleak, and windswept. As we approached Quetta the hard dry earth, dry watercourses, stunted bare trees, and a miserable dereliction of low brick buildings looked uninhabited and uninhabitable, like the ruins of a failed civilization. But there was life. The station was crowded with porters looking like refugees, gaunt Goya-like figures in long khaki over-coats and scarves, woollen caps rolled down over their ears, and knitted mittens. Outside there was snow on the surrounding hills. You soon forgot sunbathing on a cruise ship. We had arrived. As a reflection of Pakistan's friends at that time, we found our fellow "foreign" students were three Iranians, two Iraqis, two Jordanians, two Indonesians, a Sudanese, a Canadian, one American, an Australian, and a German.

If I say that we had a house and five servants in Quetta, what you might imagine will not match reality. The married quarters were single-story brick houses with flat roofs. The walls and the slab roof were uninsulated, and the walls themselves little more than one course of brick in depth. There was some reason for this apparently shoddy construction. Quetta lies in an earthquake zone, and was devastated by a severe quake in 1935. The theory, I think, was that in a major earthquake the house would collapse more easily and might not kill you. My reckoning was that the roof would do you in, but at least they could clear the site with shovels, and take the rubble away in camel carts, for excavators were not common in Quetta. We had one small quake while we were there. For a while it felt as if the world had turned to Jell-O, but it was soon over. In winter, when we arrived, the houses were arctic. Our only heating was a Quetta stove, a small squat wood burner, which had to be fed continually, or the flames died within the hour. In the summer, the interior heat could hit

120 degrees Fahrenheit by mid-afternoon. We had a living room, a small study (for I was there to work), a dining room, two bedrooms, and a bathroom. The bathroom, with its bare concrete floor, had a toilet, a sink, and a cold water pipe coming out of one wall at roughly head height. That pipe was the shower. We bathed the children in a blue plastic oversized washing-up bowl bought in the bazaar, then Janet used the same water, after which I did. Water was precious. That summer, Janet, determined to grow tomatoes in the bare sand that surrounded our house, tipped the bath water over her precious plants. She achieved, to my surprise, a bumper crop, and we shared them with our friends. It was a miracle they stayed friends. The tomatoes tasted of bath soap. They were inedible.

The kitchen, and the bare rooms that made up the servant quarters, were a place apart. There Abdul, our bearer, presided over Harry the cook, Alice the ayah, a sweeper, and a mali. The stove was paraffin, and even the hottest curry couldn't mask its stamp. On the face of it, life with five people to look after all your needs should have been domestic bliss. The reality, as Janet said, was that none of them did anything much. This was the home to which I took her when I met her at Quetta airport. Thinking to have food in the house for our evening meal, I'd told Abdul we'd have chicken that night. When we entered the house Janet was greeted by a proud Abdul and two cackling protesting hens. Each had a leg tied with twine to a leg of our dining table.

If I appear to be carping at our conditions, I am not. I am simply describing them. Our quarter, and the way we lived, served us well for a year as we changed from a one-child to a two-child family, from winter into summer, and then into the start of a second winter. It is a salutary experience to live stripped of the non-essential props we consider vital in our world. My military education ran in much the same vein. One day I wondered aloud whether we, the spoilt children of the western armies, might not be caught at a disadvantage one day. We were spending a year learning how to plan and conduct war with forces that, compared to ours, were far from rich in resources, other than manpower. My instructor overheard. He turned to me, "If you learn how to go to war with nothing, you can do anything. If you have more to do it with, you are lucky; but one day you might lose all your high-priced hardware. If you cannot win without it, what will you do then?" Fourteen years later I had to fight a war with little more than what we carried on our backs when we landed from our ships. My support helicopters had been lost when their transport was sunk, most of my vehicles had also gone down, and much of my ammunition was never offloaded. The answer was to win without it.

By the time of our first short break, the cars Tim and I had shipped to Karachi had arrived. We flew to Karachi and drove back together, in convoy, six hundred miles to Quetta. Given mobility we could make plans for our Easter break. Staying in Quetta was out of the question. We'd been to Karachi, and we'd be going there again. We'd already set a date to touch base with our greeter in Rawalpindi, and that would take us to Islamabad and Peshawar, and maybe Lahore. India was forbidden territory, for in effect a state of war existed between Pakistan and India not only in Kashmir, but in the Rann of Kutch and on either side of the Thar Desert. There was one obvious answer: Afghanistan. In a sense it was a no-brainer. At the seagull briefing the dramatic scenery of the Hindu Kush had been mentioned, as well as, in passing, the limits of our knowledge of that part of the world. As it was, Janet and I had long had two goals. I wanted to wash my hands in the Oxus (as we called it then), and she was set on collecting porcelain.

In 1767, Francis Gardner, an Englishman, was invited to establish a porcelain factory for Catherine the Great outside Moscow, charged to produce table settings and decorative pieces to rival Meissen. A hundred years later his china was famous for its beauty, form, and purity. Every Gardner bowl, if flicked with a nail, rang like glass. In time the Gardner factory expanded beyond the production of grand dinner services for the Czars to the design of wares destined for the new Russian Empire in the East. Deep red and deep blue floral patterns, "Kashgar" bowls, and green "Chinese" pattern plates. It all stopped in October 1917. From that date forward, if you were to look for Gardner china outside Russia, the terminals of the ancient trade routes, Azerbaijan, Afghanistan, and Pakistan, were the best places to find it.

It was the end of April. The Australians, Ian and Robin Mackay, with their four-year-old daughter, Kristiane, elected to ride with us. Tim and Gilly, with their two children, would leave later and join us in Kandahar. The ground clearance of the Volkswagen estate was not looking so good as we loaded the small mountain of vitals required for child support, and as many five-gallon cans of aviation gasoline as we could take. Altitude, we'd been told, would take its toll. Whatever local fuel we might find would need its octane rating boosted by a fifty percent shot of avgas, if not more. There were no child seats in those days. Somehow the young made themselves nests on soft bags squeezed between the cans of avgas, and we set off. Kabul was five hundred miles away.

We crossed a wind-blown desolate Khojak Pass and covered the eighty-seven miles to the border in fine form, but it took two and a half hours to clear the six border posts between Pakistan and Afghanistan. As daylight faded the wind stopped, and we drove northeast across the desert to the line of the Hada Hills that shielded Kandahar, then some sixty-three miles away. The road was magnificent, wide smooth asphalt sweeping across the nullahs on gently sloped concrete Irish bridges. As an aside, as the term may be unfamiliar, an Irish bridge is not a bridge. It's a river crossing, where the road continues underwater, as a ford. Hopefully it is paved, and the water no deeper than your hub caps. In times of run-off or heavy rain, your journey may well end prematurely at an Irish bridge. After the tortuous narrow shale road over the Khojak Pass, it was almost beyond belief. There was no traffic. We passed through a toll gate, paid thirty Afghanis, and by ten o'clock that night were installed in a bungalow of the Manzel Bagh Hotel outside Kandahar. There Tim and Gilly joined us and we dined on roast chicken, which was to become our staple diet. After hot showers we went to sleep with the unexpected aroma therapy of night-scented stock and geraniums, planted in row after row of flower pots on the veranda outside our windows.

Early the next day we left for Kabul. The road up the Tarnak Valley was far better than the roads of Pakistan, American-built, wide, and empty. It passed through a stony wasteland. There's a hill fort at Kalat-i-Ghilzai and an endless succession of ruined mud forts. We passed sudden rashes of black-tented nomad encampments. To the north were the distant snow-covered mountains of the Hazarajat. Somewhere along that stretch we'd stopped for a child break. Edward, in the middle of nowhere, was sitting, albeit under protest, on his blue plastic pot. A moving dot in the far distance materialized into an Afghan bus, sacks and passengers on the roof as well as inside, and about six in the cab. All were armed. The bus slowed, there were shouts as rifles were brought to bear, and a ragged salvo whip-cracked over our heads. Edward, ecstatic, leapt to his feet waving his arms, "Cwash!" (the R's were not so good then) "Bang! Cwash!" It was better than anything yet in his short life. The bus, weaving dangerously, disappeared with more shouts, and a few last shots, leaving one disappointed small boy. The show had ended as suddenly as it had started.

Two hundred and twenty miles later we reached Ghazni. Outside the town were two great shafts of brick capped by curious conical hats, making them appear like the displaced watchtowers of one of Mad King Ludwig's Bavarian castles. Whichever way you approach Ghazni, the towers draw you in like a magnet. The Towers of Victory were the eleventh century monuments to Mahmoud, founder of the Ghaznavide Empire, the man who raided India no less than seventeen times between 1000 and 1027 AD. Both of them were sadly weathered and believed to have lost half their original height, which must have been stunning. The strange conical hats were nothing but tin shields, placed above them to arrest further decay.

❖ ◆ ❖

My brief mention of Mahmoud of Ghazni is perhaps not enough. A Mongol invader, one of a long line of his kind, he was clearly taken by the geographic advantages of establishing his base in Ghazni, secure deep in Afghanistan, but close to the Khyber route into India. There, so his biographers recorded, was a land "pleasant and delightful" with "aromatic plants" and "sugar cane." It also happened to be "full of gold and jewels." The logic was that "since the inhabitants are chiefly infidels and idolaters, by order of God and the Prophet it is right for us to conquer them." Mahmoud heard the message. Seventeen rapacious trips through the Khyber netted him a fortune as well as thousands of slaves. By the time of his death in 1030 he had walled Ghazi, given it a university and libraries, and established the city as a center for astronomy, mathematics, historical research, and poetry.

❖ ◆ ❖

To one side, well apart from the two towers, the walls of Ghazni were still standing, a solid, massive shock of immense fortification from a distance, crumbling but still impressive seen at close range. Ghazni, as Major Henry Havelock said of it in 1839 during the first catastrophic British invasion of Afghanistan, was clearly a place "of great strength, both by nature and by art." General Sir John Keane, deceived by the mud forts we'd passed, lived to regret that he'd left his siege train in Kandahar. Seen at close range the city walls were clearly still strong enough to support the houses built into them, many of which were overhanging the wide dry moat around the old city. Inside the entry gate the streets were narrow, unpaved, and crowded. Shop doors, opening like caves into the mud wall behind them, were hung with posteens, jezails, scimitars, and cooking pans. Signs forbade access to the inner fortress. Ghazni soon exhausted the children's tolerance of sightseeing. We paused on the road to watch the tiny silhouetted figures of soldiers drilling beneath one of the towers, the incongruous outline of a jet aircraft, blazed into the ground like an English chalk figure, on the hillside behind them.

About a mile further on in the village of Rozah we came to the hillside park surrounding Sultan Mahmoud's tomb. We stopped. Precious water was gushing down through terraced gardens to the road, and there were malis working there, fiercely attacking the sparse weeds as if the terrible Mahmoud himself had his eye on them. Four old men were sitting on the entrance step to the tomb, which lies under a blue glazed dome. The scene was like a Persian miniature, a live stage set. All that jarred was the gaping entrance to the mausoleum. Some source I'd found stated that the missing doors had been looted, taken to Agra by the British in 1842. The reason advanced was that they were being returned, for Mahmoud had taken them from the Temple of Siva at Somnath, which he sacked in 1025. Robert Byron, who had passed that way in 1934, said the doors were rotting in the Red Fort in Agra, and the Somnath attribution was false. Mahmoud's sarcophagus, simple, plain white marble with just two lines of Kufic script, had survived without the protection of doors. In the light of the late afternoon sun, the marble glowed, translucent, against the bare stone floor. The old men, warming themselves before the harshness of the night at seven thousand feet, talked gently in the sunlight outside. We had a further ninety-three miles to run and a mini-pass to cross to reach Kabul.

What about Kabul? I can tell you what it was like then. I don't know what the war with Russia, civil war, and the massive US bombing raids of the Taliban War have left. The final stage of our journey into Kabul ran past the entrance to the green and beautiful Paghman Valley, which looked infinitely more attractive than braving the streets and traffic of an unknown city at dusk. The hills dominate every part of the city and the crowded stone and mud houses press each other up the steep slopes to join with the walls of old fortifications. Down below, the streets are a mass of shops and stalls selling sheepskins, lapis lazuli, radios and tape recorders, onyx, carpets, rifles, charpoys, cheap furniture, and tea sets.

There was the unexpected sophistication of Diana Hairdressing, and there were even supermarkets. We had nothing like this in Quetta.

In the days of Afghanistan's fragile monarchy, a new center for Kabul was to be built around the four-mile-long Darulaman Boulevard, which, straight, wide, and tree lined, was intended to rival the Champs Elysées. Amanullah, deposed in 1929, had determined to build himself a "European" capital. Nothing remained of it but the boulevard, and an immense turn-of-the-century Germanic parliament building at the far end. Unpaved tracks, that were to be radial avenues, ran off straight into stone wasteland. Not far away the few carriages destined to be the rolling stock of Afghanistan's first railway were rusting beside rails that never went anywhere. In contrast to this stillborn dream of grandeur, the old city was alive, vibrant, and an eclectic cultural mix. Letter boxes marked *Boîte aux Lettres*, tantalising glimpses of miniskirts worn under black chadris, and the sight of a Russian Gaz jeep driven by an enormous bearded Afghan, its star and sickle emblem underscored with a US Aid transfer "MADE IN USA." We stayed in the Kabul Hotel. There was nowhere else, and, hardly surprisingly, it was taken over by the Russians and used as their Headquarters in 1979. We planned to spend two nights in Kabul before setting off to see Bamiyan, Mazar-i-Sharif, and the Oxus. But it was not to be. Our time there turned into a four-day farce set on a revolving stage, in which the players were constantly changing.

On Day 2 Janet and Robin were ill, so we stayed on. Tim and I went to the palatial British Embassy, intended by Lord Curzon to be the most striking and visible proof of the power of the British Raj, to talk plans. We'd be lucky, we were told, to get to Mazar-i-Sharif and the Oxus; but no one had up-to-date information on the northern side of the Hindu Kush. Foreign diplomats and embassy staff were restricted to the Kabul area, not allowed to travel outside it without Afghan Government permission. Were we to fail to get there, Bamiyan, the Valley of the Great Buddhas, 148 miles northwest of Kabul, was suggested as another target. The Valley lies between the Hindu Kush and the Koh-i-Baba Range. The mountain passes on the way are steep, but in dry weather the roads were said to be passable.

Heavy rain fell that night. By the morning of Day 3 Tim and Ian had joined the casualty list. Robin was still sick. Gilly wanted to stay with Tim. Janet was on her feet. To our surprise, after looking at every way in which we might get to Bamiyan, we found out that we could fly to Mazar, and indeed fly from there to Bamiyan, a less than confidence-inducing venture in a Twin Otter. Janet was going to have another baby in late August/early September, and flying a hazardous, turbulent route in a small aircraft over seriously high mountains didn't appeal greatly. We decided on a day trip that day to see Jalalabad.

❖   ◆   ❖

In 1839 the British made a major attempt to take control of Afghanistan. The entry route was the way we'd come. The Bolan Pass first, staging in Quetta, then through the Khojak Pass to Kandahar, and along the road we'd taken (the only road) to Kabul. They fought their way to Kabul by way of Ghazni, and suddenly Kabul was a walkover. For two years Pashtun Afghanistan apparently accepted and became reconciled to foreign domination; then in the autumn of 1841 reality set in. The British were not welcome. The winter was hell, and soon they were in retreat, fighting a rearguard action to get to the Khyber Pass, and a battalion had been sent from India, through the Khyber, to capture Jalalabad and hold the escape route open. The ill-fated Army of the Indus was hemorrhaging in one successive action after another as it fought its way from Kabul, through the mountains, to safety. In the end only one man, Surgeon Brydon, arrived at Jalalabad, half dead, slumped in his saddle, to tell what had happened. A technically superior force, 4,500 strong (together with their twelve thousand camp followers, not least of which were their women and children), had ceased to exist. For the first time in modern history the difficulties of invading and dominating Afghanistan were demonstrated in the greatest single defeat the British Army had ever suffered.

Six years after my time in Quetta I was posted to command a battalion. One hundred and thirty-three years earlier, that unit had defended Jalalabad.

❖   ◆   ❖

Janet and I also failed to reach Jalalabad. We came close, very close, and halted. The torrential rain had washed the road away. We turned back. That night our Edward joined the Sick List. It was Day 4. The rain continued. The Kabul river was in full spate. We looked for Gardner china in the bazaars and found two "Meissen white" bowls decorated with a green, pink, and blue oriental flower design. We lunched at the Bagh-i-Bala, a white pleasure pavilion built on a hillside outside Kabul. While we were there the rain clouds broke and cleared; suddenly we could see for miles: the whole of

14

Kabul, the airport, the shell of a new Hilton Hotel then under construction, and the line of the distant Hindu Kush. Fortune was changing; we would yet cross the high mountains. That afternoon we drove to Istalif, a village famous for its local pottery, and there we discovered a minor windfall in Gardner china. The enforced delay had turned lost time to gold; and the next morning we planned to head north for the Salang Pass.

The road, like the American-built roads in southern Afghanistan, was excellent. This road was Russian, built to link Kabul with Kunduz, directly through the Hindu Kush, and shorten the distance to the Russian border by 120 miles. The Salang Pass lies about seventy-six miles from Kabul. Here the road pierces through the highest ridge in a two-mile tunnel at an altitude of just over eleven thousand feet, the highest tunnel in the world. It was a difficult but superb feat of engineering. Soon after leaving Kabul we crossed two Irish bridges running with water, a reminder of the recent rain, but otherwise the road was clear. We'd stopped at both, checked the depth, and splashed through, which the children enjoyed. Near Charikar, the peaks of the Hindu Kush became more noticeable, a snow-covered jagged wall stretching behind the bare peaks of closer mountains. After Charikar the countryside changed from the rock and stone wasteland of Kabul to the lush stepped fields of the Ghorband Valley. Not much further on, at Jabal-us-Seraj, the road left this valley to turn into the mountains, following the gorge of a tributary of the Ghorband to climb up to the Salang Pass.

Bare red hills crowned with fantastic hilltop villages overhung every twist of the road. The river, its flow controlled by barriers of concrete blocks, was a torrent of green-white water. Wherever the valley broadened slightly, tiny fields were covered in crops, and still brown ponds, fringed by willows, had orderly groups of decoys floating on them. Higher up there were no villages, and the fields had changed to patches of wet mountain grass. The trees disappeared and the protective steep brown hillsides gave way to jagged rocks and scree, and desolate isolated tombs with torn prayer flags streaming in the wind. We climbed six thousand feet in the final stages before breaking into the brilliant, intense light of open snowfields. The road ran through long galleries as you got closer to the tunnel, and the snow was packed ten feet deep between the struts of the outer walls. At the last part of the climb the road wound, still climbing under a cirque of unbroken peaks and there, a stark black hoop, was the entrance to the tunnel with its massive steel snow doors.

It was cold in the tunnel, and our car labored, even on pure avgas. There was no other traffic. We crossed the divide in the tunnel and descended towards a tiny patch of brilliant light at the far end. On the northern side there was wind, and the mountain peaks trailed horizontal snow plumes against the deep blue sky. We descended, slowly, past three gaily painted Afghan trucks grinding their way uphill, followed, even more slowly, by a donkey caravan. Below us Doshi and the northern approaches to the Salang were blanketed in cloud. Somewhere, just before or at Doshi, we had hoped to pick up the Darya-ye-Qonduz river, which, paralleling the road, ran on to Kunduz and the Amu Darya, the fabled Oxus.

We were on track. Going well. Then, short of Doshi, we were stopped at a road block. The soldiers, carrying AK-47s, were serious. Certainly not Pashtuns. Tajiks, or Uzbeks? There was something Mongolian there. Well trained. Well equipped. Uniformed. Dark green fatigues. No unit badges. No rank badges. There was no argument, and the No Go edict was absolute. We turned back, through the Salang tunnel, to Kabul. Fearful of hitting E on the seventy-plus miles where we'd seen no sign of fuel, we ran the first seventeen miles with the engine switched off. In retrospect it (1) was stupid, for we were then totally brake dependent, and (2) did not save on fuel significantly. Tim and Gilly wanted to stay in Kabul. Janet and I had a new target in mind, if we were denied the north, and Ian and Robin elected to join us.

❖   ◆   ❖

Alexander the Great spent the early part of 329 BC on the shores of the Helmand Lake, some 160 miles west of Kandahar, and recorded that he was on a great caravan route leading back to Persepolis from the Indus. He staged there because it was fertile, and it was the junction of the Helmand and the Arghandab Rivers, an area famous for its horses, and he needed remounts. By 661 AD, the time of Arab expansion, Alexander's staging post was already a great city, and then in 1150, Jahansoz, the World Burner, totally destroyed it. The city was never rebuilt. I knew little more about the place except that it had carried several names: Lashkargah, Qala Bist, Bost, or Bust, depending on your period, affinity, and native tongue. There was a US Aid project there to dam the Helmand and irrigate the surrounding desert, but the ruined city itself was largely forgotten, never explored, and never excavated. James Michener had used it as a setting in his book *Caravans*, and spoke of a great arch that rises from the ruins.

We set out from Kabul in the morning. We'd planned to spend that night at a hotel we had noted just across the Ghazni River, and stopped there to find an entrance lounge furnished with enormous, hard sofas, marble-topped tables, and tribal carpets; but that was the window dressing. Soon it became apparent there was no electricity, no hot water, no kitchen staff, and the rooms were tidy but bare white-washed cells. We decided to cook an evening meal, and drive on through the night to Kandahar, letting the children sleep in the car. And so, late that night, we returned to our bungalow at the Manzel Bagh.

From Kandahar the modern road out to Girishk, the turning point in the desert, is good. We covered seventy-one miles in an hour and five minutes, meeting almost no traffic. At Girishk we knew we had to turn south parallel to the Helmand River. The road we expected never appeared as it was shown on the map. We turned onto a track running beside an irrigation canal, checking our heading against the car compass and the distant high cliffs along the east bank of the Helmand. The surface of the track was badly corrugated and twice we waded through water. After about twenty miles the surface improved; the desert had given way to some cultivation. The improved track ran through open desert again for nearly ten miles, passing a ruined fort probably designed to command the northern approach to the city, swung down to the Helmand and crossed the river on a wide modern bridge. We were in Lashkargah, the modern settlement, the US Aid village. There were wide, gravelled, tree-lined streets, the unfenced, open house lots of suburban America with houses that looked as if they had been transported, in toto, from any southern American town, set in well-watered crabgrass lawns. Oleanders overhung the Chevrolet and Dodge trucks parked in the driveways. Somehow the alien scene, rather than being welcome, was a crashing, anti-climatic disappointment.

Then we realised that what we'd taken as the collapsed mud walls of an earlier village running parallel to the river were far more than we'd expected. The crumbled traces of walls and buildings stretched as far as the eye could see down the eastern bank of the river. We drove parallel to the river and the odometer recorded eight miles of ruins, the shells and the rubble of what must once have been forts, guard houses, and gateways. Then in the distance we saw Michener's citadel, its ochre, truncated bulk rising above the city, very much, I thought at the time, as the cathedral rises

17

above Chartres. The arch he'd written about was there, perhaps fifty feet tall, a soaring lancet curve of stone, the same line that Christian architecture borrowed from Islam. It had been restored, which quite irrationally seemed disappointing, and the steep rise of the citadel behind it minimized its height and its impact, although our car was dwarfed beneath it. But nothing could reduce the scale of those eight miles of ruined city.

The view over the southern half of the city from the top of the citadel was impressive. Sheer walls drop to the river below, and the surrounding pattern of gateways and defences stood out more clearly against the mud-colored ground. At the top of the central fortress Ian and I found a sloping, wide, brick-lined shaft, which apparently penetrated the central core of what otherwise appeared to be a solid mud hill. Vaulted arches opening into this shaft revealed two interior levels, and a broken tunnel entrance offered an apparent route deeper into the interior. We went down it, scared of hornets, scared of snakes, and close to claustrophobia. A network of beautifully vaulted brick passages opened up, some choked with rubble, others partially cleared, and then yellow hornets discouraged going much further. We reached an open room and there, squatting on the floor, digging for treasure, was an old Afghan with a Phillips transistor radio beside him.

What had he found? He burrowed in his robes, and held out his hand with a small dark stone object in his palm. It was the carved outline of a horse, about two and a half inches from head to tail, set on an integral inch of haft. The head of a knife handle? I held out my hand with money in it. He took a few Afghanis, and seemed well content. It was for the horses of Qala Bist that Alexander the Great had wintered there 2,297 years before. We salaamed, and returned to blinding sunlight. Our wives had thought they'd lost us.

As we drove away from the arch a small boy appeared out of nowhere, running beside us, begging us to stop. We did. Shyly he offered me two blackened coins about the size of a quarter. They were a pair. A head and lettering on one side, and a standing figure on the other. As with the old man (his father? grandfather?) I let him take what he wanted, and, like the old man, he was content to take just a few Afghanis. Gesturing, he made it clear the coins came from somewhere there, in the citadel.

The next day was our last in Afghanistan. Tim and Gilly had joined us the night before. We drove out to the Chilzina, the Forty Steps, a monument carved out of solid rock on the outskirts of the city. At the top is a small niche, guarded by two tiny stone lions with braided tails. In it an inscription commemorates the victories of the Emperor Babur in the sixteenth century. There, from the top, you can see all of Kandahar: the Kandahar that Alexander founded, the Kandahar of Babur, and the new Kandahar. A living timeless city surrounded by fields and trees spread like a green blanket on the desert floor. You can understand why every traveller arriving there reported it to be a minor paradise.

In July Janet and I tried once more to get to the Oxus. Now, with the distance of time and a grossly presumed increased wisdom, I cannot think why we attempted it. She was in her eighth month of pregnancy. "Heavy with child" was the only way to put it. Perhaps our move was a manic, desperate move to escape the over one-hundred-degree-Fahrenheit-plus temperatures of Quetta in summer, hoping that altitude would prove a salvation. In any event we set out. While we were in Kabul, back in the Kabul Hotel, Edward slipped on the tiled bathroom room and cut his head. Like all head wounds it bled as if the flow could never be staunched, but the skull of a child is fragile and it wasn't the blood that was worrying. The hotel staff, asked to find a doctor, were useless. We went to the British Embassy, Curzon's magnificent embassy, seeking assistance, but no one was there. It was a Sunday.

The only sensible course was to get to the military hospital in Quetta, 463 miles away. If Janet and I shared the driving and drove fast, really fast, we could make it to the border in seven hours, and reach Quetta, over the Khojak Pass, three hours later. We went like the wind, with Edward bandaged, looking like a child victim of some tribal conflict in his bloodstained turban. We reached Spin Baldak, the last Afghan border post. No, we were not allowed to leave the country. Why not? We had not got an exit permit. We remembered. The last time we had obtained exit permits in Kabul before leaving the capital. Could we get a permit in Kandahar? No, only in Kabul. Appeals met with stone walling. We had been in and out of Afghanistan before. Our passports proved it. Could we not go now? The tangled mass of red bandages and the ashen child said everything. No. The refusal was absolute. An hour of entreaty passed. It was stupefyingly hot. Edward was weakening. I could sense my temper slipping out of control.

There was just one barrier across the road, pivoted at one end, resting in a Y at the other. It was only a steel or iron pipe, but too much to take on.

It could smash the front end, maybe the windshield. Each side of it, behind the guard huts, was flat open desert. I looked at the soldiers. They were armed with cumbersome 1914 pattern Lee Enfield bolt-action rifles, Stone Age weapons compared to the automatic AK-47s of their northern kin. The weapons were dirty. Their safety catches were on. Factoring in reaction time I reckoned none of them could fire an aimed shot in under ten seconds, and achieve more than one aimed shot every five seconds after that. I doubted whether they'd had much practice at a fast moving target.

I walked a little way off the road into the desert. No one followed me for, if there was no cover, a man walked out like that to relieve himself. The desert floor was hard and could take the car, but it was rough. I worked out my course. The most dangerous part would be the stretch by the huts. If I could hit sixty we would cover that in four seconds. I might wind the car up to seventy-five by then, with luck. Back in the car we turned towards Kandahar and I drove back sufficiently far so that we would be going flat out when I left the road by the border post. The soldiers, apart from one Mongol with his rifle slung over his shoulder, had disappeared into their hut.

I turned the car around, back towards Quetta. We put our medical kit with my army field dressings, intended for bullet wounds, open on the back seat. I told Janet to hold Edward in the floor well between her legs, and crouch low. I dried my palms on my trousers and flattened the accelerator.

We were going fast. Two soldiers rushed out in panic and threw open the barrier. I thought it might be a trap, some ghastly come-on. I kept going, staying on the hard surface, accelerating. The checkpoint passed in a flash. We were in the No Man's land between Spin Baldak and the Pakistani border post at Chaman. I made Janet stay crouched, expecting shots at any moment. But none came.

Six weeks later, on 31 August 1968, our daughter Victoria was born in the military hospital in Quetta. Mithoo Minwalla, the kindest, most gentle, most fun, and most beautiful of all our Pakistani friends, said she would be her god-mother. Tim Eastwood was to be godfather. We had, by then, decided to curtail family expeditions into Afghanistan. I had, however, one last trip in mind, on which I might have to set out alone.

Two

The Road to Meshed

At the end of the year I heard that I'd been posted to the operations staff of Headquarters Northern Ireland, which came as a shock, for I'd forgotten that we had troops there. It must be a backwater, I thought. Was this the Camberley factor cutting in? In any event, we'd need our car, or a car. Sell ours in Pakistan or bring it back? Ship it, or drive it? Our successors coming out to Quetta for the next staff college course had already declined to take over our cars. The economics of paying Pakistani import duty and then selling the car were not attractive. Shipping back would take too long, months, with Suez still blocked.

I'd anticipated this. Janet and I had long had a plan on the backburner to drive overland from England to India. It seemed sensible to dig it out, and reverse it. Janet would fly back to England with Tim, Gilly, and the children. I would drive back, taking the son of the Anglo-Pakistani mission doctor with me. He had been accepted for a degree course at a technical college in London, but his mother could not afford the airfare.

I had problems. The Afghan Consulate in Quetta refused to grant me a visa. There appeared to be no reason. Was it the Spin Baldek episode? It was singularly unlikely that their immigration system, which relied on hand entries in vast ledgers, was capable of matching visa grants with entries, exit permit issues, and exits. As I'd hit a solid wall it was quit at that point, or try somewhere else. My passport traveled quite a distance in diplomatic hands, but I got it back in time, with an Afghan visa.

In ancient times there were two land routes between western Anatolia and the Mediterranean and the riches of China and India. The Silk Road would take you to China. A parallel route would take you to India. The essential difference was that the Silk Road ran north of Afghanistan. The India-bound alternative, from Istanbul through Tehran and Meshed to Herat in Afghanistan, and through Kabul to the Khyber Pass, was my way home. A continuous well-used route it might have been, for it had been in use for some five thousand years, but it was no highway, and there was no international consensus about making it so. The road ran through every variant from paved two-lane highway to dirt track. The best stretches were the American- and Russian-built roads in Afghanistan, and the road between Ankara and Istanbul. Along the route, the terrain in Afghanistan and much of Iran was desert. In Turkey it was high mountains for the greater part. Overall something like ninety-five percent of its length ran through uninhabited country. From Quetta to Istanbul the distance was about three thousand miles. At this time the main users were trucks carrying trade goods, local buses, and long-distance overland buses. These were much favored by the young who had opted out of Western civilization and were travelling east to seek Nirvana, assisted by hashish, in India and Nepal. The better heeled, and those not necessarily set on tie-dyed cotton and beads, or indeed on Nirvana, went by car.

We left on December 7. The first snow had already touched the mountains around Quetta. I was anxious to reach eastern Turkey and get through the mountain passes to the Black Sea before the first heavy snowfall there, and I knew time was against us.

❖   ◆   ❖

It was raining in Quetta as we left, and the unusually mild weather should have been a warning, a warning reinforced by minor landslides in the Khojak Pass. By the time we reached Spin Baldak the rain had set in heavily. Perhaps it was fortuitous. The interest shown by the border guards in passing traffic appeared to be near zero. After my somewhat unusual exit in July, the same car and the same driver on the same route, given the same guards, might have triggered a mental tripwire quite apart from a visa that clearly showed that it had not been issued in Quetta. As it was, the only delays we suffered were working our way through flocks of sodden, immobile sheep. In the torrential rain every animal seemed to have decided that hard tarmac was the only refuge, perhaps for lack of an ark, from the threatened flood. When we entered Kandahar, the once-green oasis was a sea of mud. Even the Manzel Bagh had lost its magic. The rain never eased.

We left Kandahar at dawn. It was still raining. We had close to four hundred miles to run to Herat, and we reckoned we'd escape the rain belt in time. Barely ten miles out, where there should have been a dry Irish bridge designed to carry the spring spate of the Arghandab River across the road, there was a three-hundred-yard stretch of fast-flowing muddy water, with an Afghan truck stalled in the flood. At that moment we should have turned back. I persuaded my passenger to wade across to see if we could ford it. The water was less than two feet deep. I lashed the flexible filler spout from one of our fuel cans to the exhaust pipe to make a crude snorkel. To lighten the car he stayed out as I crossed. Delighted with our crude snorkel, which we hardly needed splashing through four minor floods, we hammered on. We reached Herat at 12:30 that afternoon after a 380-mile run that, on reflection, was a deceptive boost to our confidence. It was still raining.

I'd long had Herat listed as a destination. In the Islamic World it had, during the Ummayad Empire of 661–750 AD, the kind of reputation and status New York has today. Based on a wide cultural diversity, it offered a center of learning, arts, entertainment, and innovation, wrapped in a far-from-fundamental tolerance of the lifestyle you might choose to adopt. Herat's decline was gradual as the lights of the Islamic Crescent faded. By the end of the nineteenth century, when the city became a part of Afghanistan, it was no more than a shadow of its past. Certainly what little remained, in terms of the provenance of a long civilization, was apparently totally destroyed by the Taliban. Like Kandahar, Herat was not looking its best in the rain. The remains of the Herat Minar with its minarets was impressive, as was the sheer bulk of the great landmark triple-towered fortress, but, again, like Kandahar, the streets and the bazaar were ankle deep in mud. Balked by the weather we gave up trying to explore Herat. We returned to our hotel and set about boiling pans of water on our Camping Gaz burner to fill bottles for the next stage of our journey. It was fortunate we did.

The next stretch, some 250 miles to Meshed in Iran, was, at any time of year, reckoned to be one of the worst parts of the overland route from Istanbul to India. There were no mountain passes to cross, but for nearly 130 miles on the Iranian side of the border the road was unsurfaced, and said to be hard going. Afghanistan offered a starting bonus, eighty-seven miles of Russian-built road leading directly from Herat to the border post at Islam Qala. We reckoned we'd stop there for the night. It was still raining when we set out. Five miles out of Herat we crossed the first bad flood, forcing the car through at speed in low gear. Further on we crossed a second flood, worse than the first, and the car nearly stalled. When we reached the third flood, over four hundred yards of water in spate, it was time to admit defeat and turn back. We decided to go to ground in Herat, and reassess our options. We snorkeled through the flood that had nearly stalled us, but exhaust heat caused meltdown in our improvised device, so we lost that option, for what it was worth.

When we reached the first flood the appearance of the torrent had changed. Before, it had been a broad width of fast-flowing dirty water; now the mud-colored surface was flecked with white-capped wavelets, and clumps of camel thorn were being carried swirling past in the torrent. As we looked at it five miserable-looking Aghans came out of a fortified mud-walled house further upstream, and stood watching us. If we were going to get across the flood, as theirs was the only habitation in sight, it seemed better to attempt it under their eyes, and ideally with their help. I reckoned weight, so that the tires would grip, was more important than buoyancy, so we both stayed on board. The first fifty yards were easy. Then the wheels slipped on a bank of silt. Water entered the heating system and a blast of steam from the demister vents obscured the entire windshield. The wheels took hold again, and the car lurched off the bank and was suddenly swept sideways by the current into a deeper channel. My crew abandoned ship. By now the waves were backing up against the side of the car to half the height of the doors, and I had the engine running at full throttle to keep exhaust pressure forcing against the water. Rocks were pounding the underneath and side of the car, and water swirled over the transmission tunnel and filled the foot wells. I heard my partner shout for help. There was no response from the Afghans. A further shout, reinforced, he told me later, by waving a wad of wet bank notes, was answered. Ten minutes later we were back on the road where we had started, just as one of the telephone poles carrying the line to Islam Qala was carried away in the flood.

It was hard to believe that it was still early in the morning. We had clocked forty-nine miles and got nowhere. The Afghans reckoned the water would abate the next day, and watched fascinated as we took advantage of a brief break in the rain to bail out the car. The rain started again, and it rained all day. Nightfall brought no change. Long before midnight it had become cold in the car, and I had to keep starting the engine so that we could use the heater to warm up for a few minutes. Above the noise of the rain on the car body was the constant roar of the torrent running in full spate across the road in front of us. Switching the headlights on it showed a swirling mass of angry brown waves. It was too wide for the light to reach the far bank, but it hardly mattered. We were trapped.

At first light the water had almost vanished, leaving vast banks of shingle and stones to mark its path. We set out for Herat, returned to the hotel we had used, had breakfast, cleaned the car as best we could, and refueled. By 8:45 we were ready to set out again. As soon as we reached our turn-back point of the day before I realized that in a day marked by my culpably bad, and arguably puerile decision making, I had made the right choice in not forcing on. After crossing over the residual debris of that flash flood the road seemed clear. The desert on each side was dull, undulating, and saturated, but at least the rain had stopped. The absence of any other traffic seemed strange, but not necessarily alarming after the weather of the last three days. The map showed only one river crossing our route ahead before we reached Islam Qala, and I reckoned we could be in Taibad, the Iranian frontier town, sometime that afternoon. Some ten miles further on I realized how wrong I was. The road cleared a crest and there, below us, it seemed that half the world was held up on either side of eight hundred yards of fast-flowing water in three main channels, with banks of shingle thrown up between the main channels. A British overland bus was stalled in the first channel, its passengers trying ineffectively to push it in any direction, and a line of cars was waiting ahead of us. One look at the water level on the side of the bus was enough to know that we'd been fooling around in play school up to that point. Most of us, eager for local reports quite apart from news of the outside world, did the rounds from car to car. A bitter north wind cut short the socializing.

At last the British bus was restarted, and heaving over the riverbed like a wounded sea monster, eventually made the crossing. A vast and dangerously overloaded Afghan truck ground its way from the far bank, almost capsizing in the deepest channel. One by one each driver screwed up his courage and forced his way across, guided by others, seeking temporary havens on each bank of shingle before risking the next channel. A party of Afghan soldiers arrived from Herat and gathered clumps of camel thorn to pad the exits. Two cars bogged down on the far side, and a Japanese girl waded the entire width of the flooded area guiding a Citroen 2CV, which sprang from bank to bank like a tiny corrugated bouncing toy. We made a mutual assistance pact with three Canadians in a battered grey

Opel. By then the best route had been proved, but it needed teamwork. We made it to the far bank.

For the rest of the distance to Islam Qala the Russian road served as little more than a general line of direction. Every nullah formed an obstacle. Each presented varying complications of deep mud, sand, rocks, and severe erosion. We learned early that it was better to detour into the desert than attempt to keep to the road. By taking the time to walk the course, it was possible to find a route across each flood channel that would take the weight of a car. We took a wide loop past an overland bus sunk axle deep in mud, with soldiers digging to free it. A second bus waited behind. Alternating the lead with the Canadians, at one point we found them stuck in a deceptively shallow gully, sinking in quicksand. We worked around so that we were ahead of them and could pull them out. Our tow rope snapped. Digging was futile as the sand flowed to fill any excavation within seconds. The pretty young wife of one of the Canadians tore her hands gathering camel thorn. We kept digging. The arrival of one of the overland buses provided vital manpower. On a second attempt the rope held, and with that and human force the car was heaved on to firm ground. By the middle of the afternoon, after diversions over stretches of desert that were hardly safe going for a jeep, we reached Islam Qala.

I reckoned Taibad, a frontier town, was likely to offer infinitely better facilities than Islam Qala, a border post, so I pressed on, for it was only twelve miles away. The Russian road ended at the border. Ended was the only word you could use. Ahead there was a morass of mud and water, a Mercedes car in the water, the piers of an unbuilt bridge, and beyond it a confusion of vehicles. A Pakistani minibus, its passengers still sorting themselves out, had apparently made it to the Afghan side a half hour or so earlier. It had taken them four days to get there from Taibad. The water, they said, was dangerous. Over three feet deep, still flowing, soft mud at the sides. Past the pool the embankment of the Iranian road was crumbling, and the road was breaking up. We returned to Islam Qala. We shared one of the six rooms in the chaikana with the Canadians. The border post doubled, and then trebled its population as the overland buses and other traffic arrived. One of the buses set off for Taibad, but was turned back by Iranian soldiers at the border. The road was closed. The main room of the chaikana was a close-pressed Babel of nationalities. Wild rumors circulated about every part of the route. Money changed hands at wildly fluctuating rates. Cigarettes, for those who had any, were worth gold. Dry wood for the fire ran out, and the place darkened with acrid wet wood smoke. Food was unobtainable. Eggs had long ran out, even nan, the staple base of every meal, was unavailable. I couldn't remember ever having felt so tired. Nothing counted, neither warmth nor food. Just sleep.

Our options were easy to define. The state of the car was the governing factor. It needed the attention of a VW agent, for the clutch, drive shaft, suspension, and brakes had taken savage punishment. The nearest agent was in Meshed, Iran. If we backtracked, there was Kabul, or Karachi. Further into Iran, Tehran. The only other route into Iran was to go back to Quetta, and take the southern desert road to Zahedan and Kerman. Zahedan was a thousand miles away by that route, and Kerman another three hundred miles of unpaved desert road. We would never make it.

We left Islam Qala early with the Canadians. The water level in the pool had reduced. We waded around, finding a course to take, and take at speed. Ten minutes later we were all at the Iranian frontier post. The next 150 miles of road were hell. At one point a convoy of nine oil tankers bound for Herat had destroyed the existing track. My companion, reserves probably exhausted, lapsed into a catatonic state. Had he been able to drive, it would have made a significant difference to my state of exhaustion, but I'd accepted his non-driving status at the start. Somewhere in those miles of dirt, stones, and severe corrugation we broke a shock absorber. A range of snow-capped mountains ran parallel to the road on the south, and the excavations for a new road ran beside us for much of the way. We envied those who would make the same journey when it was finished.

It was late afternoon when we reached Meshed. It was Ramadan. The eve of our arrival coincided with a two-day religious festival. The main streets were packed, shoulder to shoulder, with overexcited pilgrims, everywhere there were bearded mullahs, and the black flag of the Prophet hung from every house and was carried, like the battle emblem it once was, in the vast processions that formed and reformed wherever we turned. Meshed was a holy city, xenophobic and sacred to Islam. Inadvertently we broke the bounds of the imaginary zone forbidden to non-believers drawn around the shrine of the Imam Reza. Hemmed in by a mass of the faithful, we were prevented from moving further along the road. Then as our alien identity became apparent, the immediate crowd became abusive and hostile. As I tried to reverse, the first stones were hitting the car. The flames of mass hysteria were mounting second by second. The only solution was an aggressive exit. I hit the horn and surged forward, forcing those in front to leap aside in fear of their lives, slammed into reverse with the same effect, swinging the car through a ninety-degree turn. I couldn't handle the horn as well for that, then into forward, horn again, a ninety-degree turn, and we broke out, through fists, kicks, and staves, the way we'd come. Stones followed us, but mercifully a paved street, unless you break up the concrete, offers few missiles; and no windows were broken. Within two blocks we were clear.

In commercial Meshed no one would look at the car. We could drive no further. I went to the station, booked the only flatbed they had in the yard, and arranged to have the car loaded and hitched on to the nightly freight train to Tehran. I paid a porter five-hundred rials (at the conversion rates of the day, about US$7 or UK£3) to ride with it as a guard, and then booked two sleepers on the Night Express. The road journey was not over, but at least we had Afghanistan behind us.

The rest of the story is simply told. At dawn the next morning, as the train rolled out of the red desert towards the outskirts of Tehran, we saw the snow-covered cone of Damavend, beautiful against the pale sky. The headline in the English language newspaper blazed FLOOD, BLIZZARD DEATH TOLL RISES TO 45 IN PROVINCES. The article reported "The toll from floods and blizzards over the past three days yesterday rose to at least 45 dead in Fars and Khorasan Provinces and over 500 houses damaged . . . snow was reported to be falling in Meshed and other Khorasan towns paralysing life."

Three days later we left Tehran. It says much for Volkswagen that other than the starter motor and that one shock absorber, some dents underneath, and some from the Meshed stones, nothing was wrong with the car. It was serviced, it was fine, but time was against us.

Thank God I bought snow chains in Tehran, for after we'd crossed into Turkey at Bazorgan and started climbing the slopes of Ararat and the eastern mountains in a blizzard, I had to use them. My passenger, catatonic again, never got out of the car. We did over six hundred miles on those snow chains over four precipitous mountain passes, no snow clearance, no guardrails, and no other traffic, with the doors unlatched, seat belts unfastened, both of us ready to roll out the moment the car started to slide, before reaching Trabzon on the Black Sea. When we got to Erzurum, roughly the halfway point, I was so tired I drank an anaesthetizing shot of our last Pakistan Duty Free vodka and crashed fully dressed into a leaden sleep.

The rest was plain sailing. I took a detour to Bogazköy in central Anatolia to see the ruins of the capital of the Hittite Empire from 3,000 to 1,000 BC and its stunning Lion Gate. After Istanbul, I took a second side trip to see the ruins of the ten cities of Troy and stayed for one night in Gelibolu, the Gallipoli that had taken the life of one of my close forbears and so many others in 1916. I diverted briefly to Philippi. It had to be Philippi; Alexander the Great had started there.

By Christmas Eve we were in Thessaloníki, and I stopped at the Victoria Hotel, for it seemed fitting. We were the only guests. My travelling companion went to ground in his room, and I joined the owner's family for dinner and learned that he had been an interpreter in 1945 for a battalion of my regiment. The next day I crossed the Crna in sleet and snow on our way to Skopje, but feeling pressed for time, I didn't stop. In Austria, at Bad Ischl, we hit heavy snow again and the temperature plummeted to five degrees Fahrenheit. The trip mileage read 5,604 when I reached Boulogne. On 3 January 1969 we reached Kent.

In London, Spinks, the antiquarian specialists and medalists, identified the Qala Bist coins. The lettering proclaimed the head to be that of the Great King of Kings, Orthagenes, and the coins, so dated, were minted at Alexandreia Arachoris sometime around 35 to 55 AD. The city, so clearly named after Alexander, was Kandahar.

The Victoria and Albert Museum expressed a positive and unequivocal interest in our Gardner china collection, by then some twenty-four pieces, the product of the bazaars of Quetta, Kandahar, Kabul, Istalif, and Tabriz. We were encouraged to amend our wills in its favor.

The military intelligence staff in the Ministry of Defence, whose wall maps of Central Asia showed their sphere of interest, dismissed entirely my prediction that Russia would invade Afghanistan within ten years. Russian troops seized Kabul Airport on 27 December 1979, and massive reinforcements raced south to join them over the Salang Pass. I knew then that at least a quarter of a century might have to pass before any of us would be able to travel again in Afghanistan.

The Salang Tunnel, which was the vital geographic key to the Soviet invasion, was later to prove their nemesis when a convoy was ambushed there in 1987 by the mujaheddin, blocked in by fire, and incinerated. Their occupation of Afghanistan, at that point, became untenable. One final date brought the Salang Pass back into prominence. By December 2001 the terrain and the onset of winter had become critical factors in the Taliban War. Mazar-i-Sharif having fallen, Kabul became the key objective for the Northern Alliance. An advance force racing to cross the Hindu Kush was caught at the Salang Pass tunnel by the first winter blizzard and heavy snowfall. Avalanches buried both entrances. Once again that two-mile, eleven-thousand-foot tunnel became a war grave.

Four months after I had settled in my Northern Ireland backwater, the first terrorist bomb exploded. Four months later British soldiers were under fire in Belfast (as it happened not from the IRA, but Protestant extremists). As I write, thirty-three years later, the longest standing civil conflict in the Western world in the last hundred years has yet to be resolved.

One year after I had reported for duty the Army Pay Office was still struggling to come to terms with a claim for motor mileage allowance for a duty move from Quetta, Baluchistan, to Lisburn, County Antrim. They should have had no problems with it. It was legitimate, accurate, explicit, and diligently recorded in Pakistani rupees, afghanis, Iranian rials, Turkish lire, Greek drachma, Yugoslavian dinars, Austrian schillings, Deutschmarks, French francs, and pounds sterling. It also included the cost of three ferry crossings: the Bosphorus, the English Channel, and the Irish Sea.

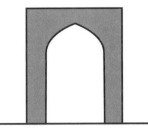

Pakistan

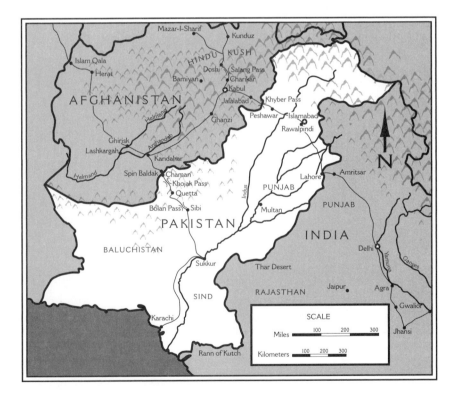

Three

The Wedding Season

Twenty-one years had elapsed since I had left Pakistan to make my way back to England overland. I had not returned to Pakistan, although Janet and I had been twice to India, forbidden territory when we were living in Quetta. Our Indian visits, both for pleasure and research, had covered much of the north, and with less delight, Calcutta, Madras, and Mumbai (Bombay, as it was still called at that time). Now we were back in Pakistan, in Karachi, with Victoria. We were there to honor a long-standing promise to show Victoria the country of her birth, and we were there, at the invitation of her Pakistani godmother, Mithoo Minwalla, to join her in attending a series of weddings and parties, for it was the wedding season.

At that time a brief rapprochement between Pakistan and India had led to the opening of the land frontier between Lahore and Amritsar. If ever there was a chance to cover that handspan stretch of the Grand Trunk Road it was at that moment, and, if we were opportunistic and went that way, Janet and I could show Victoria Delhi, Agra, and Fatehpur Sikri. My original plan had been to travel more widely in Pakistan, to take Victoria back to her birthplace in Quetta, but not then—not in the bitter cold of a Baluchi winter, not six thousand feet up on that bleak plateau on the borders of Afghanistan where the snow on the surrounding peaks was probably waist deep.

I confess that I had my own agenda in India. During our earlier travels I had lost both heart and mind to a stunningly attractive young woman, the widowed child bride of an Indian ruler. She was Lakshmibai, the Rani of Jhansi, who had died in action fighting the British in 1858. When Janet and Victoria returned home, I would stay in India, find her shadow, and follow her footprints. But first, this is Karachi. As I touch on geopolitics, I would remind the reader that the date is late December 1989. My chapters follow sequentially up to 1990.

Although not germane to my account, perhaps I should add that by then I had retired from the army, and Janet and I were living in the United States, as indeed was Mithoo Minwalla.

The whole city is the color of dry dust. Pavements, walls, houses, and the few trees look as if rain had never fallen, and the sky is the color of an old blue cotton shirt, bleaching to whiteness in the harsh haze of noon. Karachi is not attractive. It was even less attractive than I remembered it. The public urban infrastructure, streets, drains, utilities, parks, and public buildings are monuments to the skill and probity of their British builders for maintenance is minimal. Why, you ask yourself, is there a total absence of environmental pride, order, cleanliness, and a dedication to renewal? The manpower is there. Is it a lack of direction and discipline? Ignorance? Apathy? Incompetence? Does it matter? Over a millennium probably not, and who cares for Karachi anyway? It was an alien creation, a series of muddy fishing villages at the mouths of the Indus converted by the British into a seaport in case something went wrong in Bombay. Even worse, it is Sindhi territory, and who would hold any brief for the Sind? None, if you are Punjabi or Pathan. Karachi is a long way from Lahore and Rawalpindi.

If you are rich, the fortress home is the way you survive. We lived that way in Europe in the Middle Ages. High walls, barbed wire, and iron gates surround your territory. Your chowkidars man the gates but if you are important, armed police will be there, too. Inside the walls you have malis to make perfunctory attempts at gardening, and a whole retinue of house servants to attend to your needs. With great kindness we were accepted as guests at the house of the godmother's aunt who lived on Victoria Road in a perfect period piece of late Colonial architecture: cavernous high-ceilinged square rooms that reduced monumental furniture to doll's house miniatures, great primitive bathrooms floored and walled in white marble, and wide verandas. We rattled round a bit in our echoing empty spaces but were well attended by a retinue considered modest by any standard: a bearer, just one house boy, a sweeper, two chowkidars, two malis, a driver, a cook, two servant girls, an old ayah, a night ayah, and a clutch of children who acted as gophers and assistants to them all. Every day new red and white chalk symbols were drawn with painstaking care on our doorsteps and on the walls by the main doorway, flowers, and hearts, and fishes, in pairs, reversed, like yin and yang symbols.

Nine weddings took place in the four days we were there, lunches every day and two receptions an evening. It was January, the wedding season, nothing was unusual. Why January, you might ask? Rather like June in England, or New England, it's the weather factor, and it's the favorite month. The best month. If you chose June in Karachi, you'd regret it, for June, July, and August are the monsoon season, hot (95 to 115 degrees Fahrenheit), humid, and maybe wet. At the top strata of society, those are the months you go to Europe. In winter Karachi is entirely tolerable, with temperatures sixty to eighty degrees Fahrenheit, and it's dry. It's a time when the fair sex can dress to the nines, changing two or three times a day, rarely repeating an outfit or jewelry. Even hands are painted in henna with exotic patterns, which can takes hours to complete. It's a time when you can entertain vast numbers outside, in the open air, or under decorated canopies. It's a time of endless small talk, endless greetings and standing around, and you are lucky to eat by 11 at night or to see your bed before 2:00 am. You embark on this social marathon without the kick-start or sustenance of alcohol, for Pakistan is a consciously Muslim country, but forewarned is forearmed.

We were changing one evening. I had just poured two inches of vodka into our tooth mugs, ready for the 7-Up that Janet had bought from a stall across the road, when the servant girl Lakshmi, known as "Alice," entered without warning looking stunning in her best yellow shalwar kameez, picked up the two glasses, emptied them into the basin, washed the glasses perfunctorily under the cold tap and left, her early evening duties done. At that rate our duty free stock would never last until we reached India. But the prohibition was almost as casual as it had been when we lived in Pakistan sixteen years before.

A Parsee guest, with the distancing of another faith, commented "They all drink. No one, being Muslim, dare admit it or drink in public, but in their own houses or in your house they will all drink. You can buy all the liquor you want anywhere in the bazaar. An ordinary bottle of Johnny Walker Red Label will cost you a thousand rupees (about $50 or £30). You just have to pay. That's all." We were drinking Red Label then, the men together, while the women, restricted to orange juice, were prisoners in a begum's corner (the women's side of the social sexual barrier). Janet, although conditioned to it by our earlier existence in Pakistan, later wished an unmentionable fate on Alice for the loss of her two inches of precious vodka earlier that evening. The next night was exceptional. Prohibition was enforced.

"Tonight we can't drink." Our host was apologetic and clearly put out by the limitation placed on his ability to entertain as he wished. "There are three reasons. The Chief Minister is here, and he can't be seen where there is drinking. And the Begum is here. There are too many people here (the guest list was over a thousand), and some of them might object. And the police are all around." Which they were. Guarding us all in our shamianas, our gilded party tents. So we were all reduced to orange juice and political comment.

"As soon as someone is elected [as President], first of all they wipe out the opposition, and then they wipe out the opposition in their own party. The only way this will change is if they lose a war, then the other guy comes in. The new one comes in and everyone thinks they are wonderful. But exactly the same cycle starts again . . ."

"Democracy can never work."

"They are killing anyone. It never was like this. And it is always the innocent who die."

It's standard talk. It means little. You are in a country where an aristocracy founded on land, industrial, and commercial wealth has survived, and will survive. The top twenty families are educated, urbane, westernized, have bank accounts in Geneva, buy designer dresses in Paris, their suits in London, and know their way into any one of the best restaurants in Manhattan. The real problems remain unaddressed. Pakistan's relationship with India, unresolved since the Kashmir dispute, the inconclusive 1965 War, and its defeat in 1971. Its ambiguous position with China, courted to frighten India, and Iran, courted for Muslim clout. How do they stand with Afghanistan, after two decades of conflict there? There's only one answer and that is "decidedly uneasy." In government circles the popular myth is that military strength equals security; but it must be, and is, transparently clear that the staggering cost of maintaining Pakistan's conventional armed forces, and covertly trying to build a nuclear arsenal into the bargain, will inevitably exacerbate every social problem (and in Pakistan the list is endless). What follows? Predictable political failure, and ultimately the intervention of the Army into the political arena, if not actual military rule.

The problems are bad enough as they stand. They become intractable overlaid with the dead hand of Islamic fundamentalism. It's not the trivial issues, such as the prohibition of alcohol. It's the dead weight of a medieval religion geared to strictures of prohibition, prosecution, xenophobic suspicion, and censorship. The mullahs of today are far removed from the gentle world of Akbar's tolerance. No religion is tolerable when it is imposed on others, when it directly governs the life of others, whether they are a part of it or not. The blind bigotry, the myopia of fundamentalist Islam, is beyond understanding. Pakistan, in the final decade of the twentieth century and to date, into the twenty-first century, rates the evidence of a woman in legal cases as half that of a man. If a woman accuses a man of rape, the automatic assumption is that she is guilty of enticement. She will be beaten for provocation and imprisoned for two years, a mandatory sentence, unless four independent male witnesses can state in court that she did not entice her assailant. The extreme punishment of stoning to death remains on the statutes. It was Pakistan that made its female athletes in the All Asia Games compete clothed from neck to ankle in shalwar kameez regardless of their sport. A country that professes to owe everything it cherishes to the early Moghuls really needs that second Akbar; but I doubt that a graduate of Quetta will ever fit the bill.

Democracy can never work? When I asked, somewhat hesitantly, why it might not be attempted, I was told categorically that it would be impossible. The people were too stupid. They had no education. They knew nothing, nothing at all.

Between the dressing up and the parties we wandered around the bazaars, and in one small shop devoted to Baluchistan onyx, I found a tiny carved terrapin, barely an inch and a half long. I bought it at once. At that time, in England, I had a twenty-six-foot center cockpit catamaran under construction in Cornwall. Her lines, with a turtle back formed by the coachroofs of the fore and aft accommodation, diminutive size, and the twin hull capability of being able to sit happily on a beach, had led me to name her *Terrapin*. I was to take delivery the next year, in March 1990, and in staged journeys over three years take her south to the Mediterranean, across the Atlantic to the Caribbean, and northwards to her destined home in Florida. The little onyx terrapin, by then mounted on board in a frame of Vermont cherry, was her lodestar in some seven thousand nautical miles of voyaging.

In one of our breaks from the partying I went to the National Museum. It was not impressive at first sight, set in a desolate garden park crossed by ruined garbage-filled water channels, a few decaying palms; the rest was trash and filth. A sign in the entrance proclaimed:

God effaceth and establisheth what he pleasesth

which seemed a touch heavy-handed. Sententious? Certainly it was hardly welcoming. To my secret delight it had been complemented by a second line in carefully matched lettering:

be a hell of a sight better if Man got a grip

I wanted to look at some Kafiristan wooden statues, which I believed were there. I was interested in early human images made with inlaid eyes, a trail I'd been picking up intermittently on other travels, having become fascinated by Thor Heyerdahl's thesis on the lineage of the moai, the giant statues in Easter Island. The Kafiristan figures were there, looking a little tired and dusty, but they had onyx eyes and top knots, and looked like small protoypes of their distant cousins on Easter Island. I was no wiser about their origin, date, and purpose, there was no explanatory card, and no one to question; but if nothing else it was a check mark on my Things To Do list.

On our last day in Karachi we decided to go crabbing. I can't remember why, and in truth I can't think why we did it, save that crabbing has long been a traditional Karachi recreational pursuit. The crabbing boats look as if they'd been imported from Egypt during the Middle Kingdom with their broad, solid decks, lateen rig, cotton sails, and home-spun hemp rigging. The wind was against us and we had no engine, so we were towed away from the dock by a fishing boat that was leaving at that moment. Minutes later we crashed into a water taxi, caromed into our towing vessel, and within seconds became the center of a three-boat, mid-channel tangle. Our all-family crew—grandfather, son, and nine-year-old grandson—were quite unperturbed by it all and continued to squat on their hunkers, sorting out their fishing tackle. Eventually we made the outer reaches of the harbor and anchored near a dredger, thanking our tug, which went on towards Manora Point and the open ocean. The ebb tide swung us around and swept past us, opaque green water carrying the sewage of Karachi and the scourings of a thousand miles of the Indus River. I vowed I wouldn't touch anything we caught as the boy baited hooks with fish heads and handed us our lines.

By the time we pulled in the first crabs grandfather already had a dechi on a paraffin stove and was frying onions as he stirred in curry powder, and a second cooking pot on another oil stove near the boil, ready for rice. The curry absorbed tomatoes and quartered potatoes, and then the first crabs were added to it. By the end of an hour the meal had been built into a large pot of crab soup, with rice on the side, together with additional crab claws and pieces of stir-fried crab. We all crouched around the full pots, loaded our Chinese enamel soup bowls to the brim, and tucked in. I could see cholera on the horizon, as clearly as I could see the pattern of painted chrysanthemums emerge into the glare of noon at the bottom of my empty bowl, but it tasted better than a three-star bouillabaisse made from the pick of the catch of the day.

Two bowls later we sailed off slowly downwind, hardening up into a broad reach. We were moving quite handsomely by then and passed under the quarter of HMS *Coventry*, perhaps cutting it a touch fine, but they hardly gave us a glance. It crossed my mind to put about and call on her, but we were still washing the dishes and perhaps not looking our best. We sailed on, leaving the anchored warship and some twenty other ships, all anchored in the outer reaches of the harbor, far behind us. If you ever miss sighting the Manora light, the fleet of anchored, waiting ships is the certainty that you've reached Karachi. About two thirds of the harbor handling equipment is out of order, container gantries are desperately needed, and there's little in the port that is still running or working as it should. It takes days to load or unload a ship. The waiting period alone, before you get your turn, can be measured in weeks; and Karachi is Pakistan's sole seaport. Not bound by this interminable call-forward rota we took our final run in style as if the binoculars of the Cowes Committee were on us and, with the nine-year old nipping about with old car tires, his father at the main sheet, and his grandfather at the helm, came alongside our departure dock in as neat a controlled crash as you have ever seen.

A rash of banners and posters in Urdu and English had gone up while we were out of Karachi:

ANYONE STAGING PARTIES TO CELEBRATE NEW YEAR DOES SO AT THEIR OWN RISK

Who was behind it? No one seemed to know. Muslim fundamentalists was the general opinion. The international hotels had been called and told that they would be bombed if they stayed open on December 31. Every four- and five-star hotel took the threat seriously. All dinner reservations were canceled. The entire police force and the auxiliaries were mobilized and suddenly Karachi was full of armed men.

Police cordons were around the hotels, roadblocks were imposed, and if you got into a hotel, you couldn't even get a cup of coffee. Even the coffee shops were closed. We were left with a party and nowhere to go. That evening we decided to drive out to Clifton, Karachi's seaside suburb, to see if we could escape the shutdown. Clifton, dreary at the best of times, consisting for the most part of deteriorating, shoddy, newly-built, untenanted apartment blocks, rough unfinished pavements, and poorly lit roads, was deserted. Three Chinese restaurants were open. We tried the best looking one. It was garishly decorated, the food was poor, and the place was, of course, unlicensed. When we left the restaurant the street-lights had been turned off.

We drove back to Karachi to be caught up in a cavalcade of what we took to be New Year celebrants, all male, crammed into overloaded cars, riding in twos and threes on motorcycles, and clinging to trishaws, all set on streaming out of Karachi on the Clifton Bridge. Every lane was blocked. Tension was high. Slowly we made our way along Khayaban-e-Iqbal where we ran into a major police roadblock outside the Pearl Continental. We were hemmed in by traffic and by a near-solid mass of highly excited males. No females were in sight. A bus was stopped at gunpoint and a man dragged off it and severely beaten, on the spot, by the police. We had the windows up, the doors locked. Janet, Victoria, and her godmother were crouched, out of sight, below window level. We heard the first shots. Sensing the chance to make the softest landing ever after a shallow dive, I flattened myself on a bed of three protesting females, squashing them into the floorwells. Janet was vocal. It was fireworks. There were ragged volleys all around us. The sharper whip-like crack of bullets passing overhead lent some encouragement to maintaining a low profile. No mistake. There were no starbursts in the sky, and I knew that sharp crack. It was rifle fire.

Somehow we got out of the jam and found refuge in a friend's apartment nearby until about 1:30 in the morning. The fireworks, by then, had settled into long bursts: light machine guns, or assault rifles set on automatic. The firing became sporadic, and sensing a temporary lull or the exhaustion of the warring factions, we made it home.

The morning newspapers were less than forthcoming.

BLAST THREAT SCARES REVELLERS

was the headline of the day. We read that a Sub-Inspector of Police and three others, two shopkeepers and a fisherman had been shot the day before. That was it. Almost inexplicably a curfew was announced as being in force in Malir, Malir Extension, and Model Colony from 10:00 pm that night until 7:00 am the next day. Oh yes, and water supplies were to be restricted in some twenty areas of Karachi. The system had broken down. The Dawn leader was optimistic. Under a color photograph of a woman lighting a hurricane lamp was the exhortation:

> **Every New Year is an invitation to hope—the eternal lamp that lights the path through the thick mists of uncertainty and the unknown. For an individual, as for a nation, hope is a risk well taken when looked upon as a sustainer and fortifier of human struggle for progress and betterment.**

It was a pity the hurricane lamp was rusty, which showed plainly in the color print. It was also unfortunate that the lamp's fuel filler cap had been lost and the orifice was stuffed with a piece of rag. The lady with the matches was hanging on in there, taking hope as a risk.

But who was fighting whom? I could guess, but I never learned the truth. Karachi's population was a volatile mix. Its start point was polyglot. The original Sindhis, mohajirs (Muslims who fled from India at the time of Partition in 1947), and Punjabis. The business of government was

41

essentially in Punjabi hands. This was complicated in the 1980s by a floodtide from Afghanistan: refugees and exhausted mujaheddin, escaping the Russians and running from the civil strife that gave rise to the Taliban. These last migrants were armed. Add rising Islamic fundamentalism, and what do you get?

For the first time in years, ever since Pakistan and India had been bent on mutual destruction, the land route between Lahore and Amritsar had been declared open. There were drawbacks to this apparent attempt to return to normality, however. You had to cross the border on foot, no vehicles were allowed, and the rail link remained severed. But if nothing else, in theory at least, you could now travel the Grand Trunk Road from the Khyber Pass to Calcutta. We thought we'd enter India that way, fearing that if we missed this window of opportunity, it might never occur again. We'd work out the final detail on the ground, but the first stage was to get to Lahore. By air. Any other route would take too long. It was not looking so good. Between December 17 and the end of the month, 80 flights to Lahore had been canceled and 250 were delayed. There was a log jam of backed-up bookings. We had no alternative but to switch to the train, but then, providentially, at the last minute a well-placed friend intervened and got us the air tickets we wanted.

We were fortunate. The train we would have taken was purposefully derailed on the main Karachi–Lahore line in the Sind Desert just north of Sukkur. When rescue workers reached the scene they found the surviving passengers were not just shocked, but the victims of inhuman banditry. If rings and bangles could not be taken easily, the robbers had amputated the fingers and hands of the 307 travellers who had died, and the 700 plus who were injured, to take their spoils.

Four

Crossing the Divide

He sat, in defiance of municipal orders, astride the gun Zam-Zammah on her brick platform opposite the old Ajaib-Gher—the Wonder House, as the natives call the Lahore Museum. Who hold Zam-Zammah, that "fire breathing dragon" hold the Punjab; for the great green-bronze piece is always first of the conqueror's loot.

There was some justification for Kim,—he had kicked Lala Dinanath's boy off the trunnions,—since the English held the Punjab and Kim was English. Though he was burned black as any native; though he spoke the vernacular by preference, and his mother-tongue in a clipped uncertain sing-song; though he consorted on terms of perfect equality with the small boys of the bazar; Kim was white—a poor white of the very poorest.

The opening lines from *Kim*. Rudyard Kipling, 1901. His epic story of the North West Frontier, of espionage, and the "Great Game" of great power rivalry.

 It was early morning. Lahore had vanished in the near-zero-visibility mist rising from the Ravi River. On the banks of the Bari Doab Canal the letter writers, wrapped in their dhotis against the morning chill, looked like mummies crouched over their ancient typewriters, part silhouetted by the flickering charcoal fires of the food sellers. The whole scene was the stage set of fantasy, a world made even more bizarre by the incongruous, skeletal mass of Kim's gun, the great gun Zam-Zammah, set against the backdrop of the Lahore Museum.

The humongous Zam-Zammah, its barrel longer than two six-foot men, with a gaping muzzle large enough to swallow the head of a young child, was said to have been cast, with a twin, by the Afghans in Lahore in the early 1760s. At that time the city was in their hands. The two huge guns were taken back to Afghanistan, but the twin sank in the Chenab River on the way back. Zam-Zammah was used in battle a year later at Paniput on the Grand Trunk Road, about fifty-seven miles north of Delhi, where an invading Afghan force defeated a Mahratta army. Nearly a hundred years later, Zam-Zammah, by then in Sikh hands, saw action for a second time at Multan. This city, some two hundred miles to the southwest of Lahore, had long shared with it the guardianship of the northern plains of India. Alexander the Great had faced delays there during his bid for India. In 1848 the British, also bent on take over, found no welcome mat laid out in Multan. The city, with Zam-Zammah, held out under siege; but a year later the overriding strength of the invading force dictated surrender. The great gun was eventually set outside the Lahore Museum as a landmark, and a curiosity, by the British governors of the Punjab.

Zam-Zammah was famous in its own right, and has been famed since the 1901 publication of *Kim*, as "Kim's Gun." I know of no more engaging and magical book of India, and of the British Raj, than Kipling's *Kim*. It is a wonderful, vibrant story, and I use my words advisedly.

Perhaps I should explain "letter writers?" In a country where much of the population was illiterate, and communication by telephone was not an option, the letter writer served a vital need. Through his services you could dictate a letter to your relatives who might have moved elsewhere, while they, writing through him, could stay in touch with you. Once a common feature of Indian street life, my impression is that schooling there, even in rural areas, has made the letter writer largely redundant.

We held our lives in our hands even standing on the sidewalk. The early morning traffic was manic, murderous. Trishaws, buses, taxis, and trucks fought for every inch of road space with pedestrians, bicyclists, gharris, and camel carts. With fifteen-yard visibility it was bedlam. We'd set out, on foot, for the walled city. Forced into a taxi in self defense, we were carried with the mainstream only to stop, with rear-ending abruptness, gridlocked near the Lahore Gate. There we stayed for ten minutes, jammed between a heavily overloaded gaudily decorated truck and a horse pulling an equally overloaded flatbed cart. It was not the best of places to be trapped. The mouth of the horse was torn by a crudely made ill-fitting bit, which had stripped the flesh from its lower jaw to leave nothing but exposed teeth and jawbone. When the traffic jam eased, the mist had cleared. It was getting hot, which didn't help when you were feeling sick, and close to retching.

Talk of the great cities of the Moghuls, and Lahore is right there, one of the top three on your list (along with Delhi and Agra). As ever, much of the history starts with forts, and the one name that heads the list of epic builders is Akbar, the third emperor. Make no mistake, for him Lahore was no green field site. It had been fortified for a thousand years before he came that way. But it was Akbar (log his Lahore residence as 1584 to 1598) who decided on a tear-down job and a rebuild, and the result was, and is, stupendous. The centerpiece, and citadel, of Akbar's "new" walled city with its twelve gates was, of course, Lahore Fort. On the banks of the Ravi, and on the Grand Trunk Road, you could call it the gateway to all the riches of India. We entered the fort through the Shah Burj Gate, the emperor's private entry, up the stepped ramp that was called the Elephant Path. High above us on a frail bamboo ladder a man with a flaming torch was attacking a bees's nest, unprotected save for his round sunglasses and a scarf tied under his jaw and knotted on the top of his head. Apart from the dark glasses and his immediate occupation, he looked like a Cruickshank caricature of an eighteenth century sufferer from toothache. It was a bizarre start.

Akbar's main entrance, the Masjidi Gate, is largely untouched, but nowhere in Moghul India, save for Fatehpur Sikri, do you expect to find pristine unchanged Akbar architecture. Every emperor after him, Jehangir (1605–1627), Shah Jehan (1627–1658), and even the fanatical fundamentalist Aurangzeb (1658–1707) added his modifications. It was so in Lahore, and it was so in Delhi, and in Agra. His successors did well; some of their work is stunning. Lahore Fort had not been in good shape when Janet and I first saw it in 1968; and twenty-two years later, by the time we finished our tour, I wished we hadn't returned there. The dereliction was worse. Shah Jehan's Diwan i Am, the Hall of Public Audience, had lost all but its basic dimensions, his quadrangle was close to ruin, the Diwan i Khas, the Hall of Private Audience, was in a sad state, and so was his Shish Mahal, the Hall of Mirrors. On the west side of the Fort the one contribution you would have expected from Aurangzeb, a mosque, is there, and splendid. The Badshahi Mosque is arguably the best of its kind ever built. But the climax was spoilt; the Alamgiri Gate, a clip-on enhancement, added to give access to his mosque through a garden courtyard, was in decay and fouled by garbage.

The Sikh wars of the 1840s were the start of this downslide. It was accelerated by British vandalism. The central fountain in Jahangir's quadrangle was destroyed to make a tennis court. His bathhouse became a kitchen. A Shah Jehan pavilion was "made over" into a church. So it went on. There were many such traumatic changes. I had hoped, against all hope, that Pakistan might at last have embarked on a restoration program that would have set Akbar's fort rightfully back in its place in the front rank of colossal Moghul architecture, alongside the Red Fort in Delhi and the Red Fort at Agra. There were some indications of perfunctory maintenance, but only Akbar's massive construction had so far saved Lahore Fort from crumbling to rubble; no major work had been carried out that would count as restoration, let alone museum-quality care. We'd carried Victoria, just four weeks old, around the fort in our arms when we were last there. If there was any way in which I could breathe some magic for her into the land of her birth, and a sense of the triumph of the Moghuls, the chance should have come in Lahore. It never did.

We left to take a taxi out on the Grand Trunk Road to the Shalimar Garden. It had been in poor shape when Janet and I were there on that 1968 visit, which had saddened Janet, for gardening is her delight. Shalimar, Shah Jehan's paradise, was one of the first and the greatest of the Moghul gardens, the precursors of many of the formal gardens in Europe. That day I'd taken a photograph of a seated Janet in the garden, focussing on her and not the threadbare grass and weed-choked flower beds. She had a silk square tied in a triangle over her head, in the way it was done in the fashion of the sixties, and was cradling Victoria on her lap. Edward, just two years old, was looking down at his sister, still trying to work out who, or what, she was. There was something in that one frame as there sometimes is, a fleeting moment that film can catch if you're lucky, but the human retina can never freeze. Janet had bent momentarily over the little girl and, with her head bowed she was, that instant, a Mantegna madonna.

Shalimar was in worse shape than it had been in 1968. Maybe the magnitude of restoring Lahore Fort is beyond expectation, but the Shalimar Garden could be restored to all its glory. It had become no more than a walled amusement ground for groups of loud-mouthed ill-mannered youths. There was litter on the lawns and in the water channels; the shalimar itself, the water cascade of lights, was stained and dirty; the marble of the fountains was dirty and defaced by graffiti; and fires had been lit in the Hall of Private Audience. Were I Pakistani, I vowed then, I would seek to have the garden closed for eighteen months, which is the time it took Shah Jehan to have it built, have it restored totally, policed properly, and used for festivals and son et lumière as a tangible, visible, symbol of pride. Yes, pride in my nation, which, after all, was established for no other reason but to foment Muslim (and in that read Moghul) pride. But Pakistan had lost the plot. If you think of the triumphs of the Moghul architecture and Moghul gardens now, you think of India.

We were thinking of India. We were staying in Lahore at Faletti's, which was like living in a seventeenth-century serai with its arcades, fourteen-foot rafted ceilings, immensely thick walls, and an endless succession of room boys, waiters, and helpers in constant attendance. Regardless of the sense of time warp, we had all the right facilities. There was hot and cold water, a vast bathtub set in a pink tiled surround that could have served to bathe small elephants, and a virulent lilac toilet, which worked, if you took the lid off the cistern. It was comfortable there, and the uncertainty of the unknown can make a powerful incentive for staying put. It's no more than eighteen miles from Lahore to the border, and if we'd stayed on the Grand Trunk Road, and kept going past the Shalimar Garden, we would have reached the divide. We were going to go that way, for we had this one unique window of opportunity to cross the land border between Pakistan and India. But we stayed on in Lahore for one more night. It was not fear of the unknown. It was disappointment. A disbelief that our time in Pakistan had ended so negatively, and a childlike hope that somehow, if we just stayed on one more night, somehow, magically, the rabbit might come out of the hat.

In my first chapter I touched on geography and the routes between Afghanistan and India. Of the two "drop down" passes from the high country to the riverine borders of ancient India, I much prefer the Bolan. It matches your expectations for it looks like a pass, feels like a pass, and it's long, tortuous in part, and dramatic. The Khyber, with terrain more open than the defiles of the Bolan, may be a disappointment as a photographic target, but for the conquerors it hit the spot as the way to go. Once you were through the snake bends, you were heading in the right direction. It was as easy to follow the Grand Trunk Road as it was to take the Yellow Brick Road to Oz, for Lahore, Delhi, and Agra were right there, in line, in front of you.

Travel, for me, would lose much of its allure if I didn't know who had been that way before, and possibly contrarily, I tend to favor unfrequented routes, and oddball approaches. Earlier I mentioned Semiramis, Queen of Assyria, in connection with the Bolan route. The details of her bid for India are as astounding as the early date, some three thousand years ago, but she had the resources to make it. The Assyrian Empire (950 to 612 BC) had just about the whole of the Near East sewn up, with what are now Syria, Lebanon, Israel, Palestine, Jordan, and Iraq as one territory, centered on present day Iraq. Spearhead of a superpower as she was, none the less she found, as others found later, that if you took the Bolan, you ended up on the banks of the Indus, mid-river, with the Thar Desert in front of you. Your river crossing problem was more than doubled that far downstream, and if you got across, what were you going to do? Hike across the desert to get to anywhere worth getting to in India? But that may not have been immediately apparent.

Only two problems preoccupied this remarkable woman. The first was the size of the Indus. You needed boats, real boats, to cross it. The second was the pure terror induced by the first sight of Indian war elephants, beasts the like of which had not been dreamed of in her part of the world. Nothing if not resourceful, she sent to Phoenicia and Cyprus for shipbuilders and had pre-fabricated craft built and transported overland, with their makers, to join her expedition. The elephants were quite another problem. At her command 300,000 oxen were killed and their hides used, stretched over framework, to construct the most enormous beasts, which were to be powered by camels harnessed inside the hollow shells. With all the boat building and animal fabrication, it took three years to get this extraordinary invasion force ready to move forward again.

The boats served them well. The Assyrians crossed the Indus and then the fighting had to start. Right up in the vanguard of Semiramis's army the make-believe monstrous beasts were pushed and dragged forward as their built-in camel power proved inadequate. Their desired shock effect, a masterstroke in blitzkrieg, never materialized; somehow, the news had got out that appearances were not everything. The morale and motivation of the men and camels sewn into the mammoth mock-ups, all of whom must have been hyperventilating and half dead from heat exhaustion, could not have been high. Even worse, it soon became apparent that the Indian war elephants were less than impressed by their rivals. After one stumbling charge the invasion turned into a rout, and one report has it that Semiramis died in the confusion. I hope not, for her inventive talent and determination deserved a better end. Hardly surprisingly, the Khyber became the popular route.

Alexander the Great headed for India via the Khyber. He too was balked by the last of the five rivers. The Greeks, by then, had faced a lot of splashing around on river banks, which is always a dangerous activity for soldiers who don't normally take kindly to boating. His men were now a long way from home, and, rather like the over-heated Assyrians trapped with the camels inside the mock elephants, their hearts were not in it. Standing on the banks of that last river, with all of India before them, his men mutinied.

The Grand Trunk Road, already an established caravan route, passed back into the hands of the traders. It came back into style as an invasion route around 600 AD with a bizarre and discomforting succession of invaders. White Huns, Iraqis, and the first of the newly thrusting Afghans, Mahmoud of Ghazni, whose tomb we'd seen at Rozah, and then the Moghuls. By the start of the sixteenth century Akbar the Great had set a pattern for living that could be copied to advantage by the nations today dedicated to ethnic monoculture and the hegemony of a single faith. The "Grand" in the name of the route was a misnomer, but this single narrow road, barely a two-lane highway, was a vital artery that had served the Moghuls, the British, and trade and human communication for centuries, its utility as a siphon for invasion causing no more than a temporary delay in traffic.

When the Grand Trunk Road was cut, and severed completely by the Partition of India in 1947, it was traumatic. Today, more than fifty years later, we are all held to ransom by the consequences.

It's three miles from Lahore to the Shalimar Garden, and then you have fifteen miles to run to the border. At first the road is alive, filled with traffic, as is every road in Pakistan and India, and the conventional rule, as ever, remains that the largest vehicle on the crown of the road, regardless of direction of travel, has the right of way. The exhilaration, just riding as a passenger in a taxi, can lead to cardiac arrest. So it was that morning, and then suddenly adrenalin was no longer vital, for the road was like a drying river, nothing was coming our way, and almost no one was going our way. Then it was deserted. We entered an empty frontier zone of untilled fields, army posts, and barbed wire. At the first Pakistani border post we could go no further, except on foot. Twice our names and personal details were painstakingly entered by hand into great ledgers. Slowly we were moved from checkpoint to checkpoint, surrounded by customs officials, soldiers, armed police, and immigration agents. Then we were pushed out with our suitcases through a high gate into the unknown, and the gate locked behind us. We were on the Grand Trunk Road, empty of all traffic. The surface, obviously serving no useful purpose, was not so good. You don't need directions. You walk. Following the road. We walked five hundred yards through a No Man's Land carrying our bags, and arrived, again through a gate in another border fence, which was opened as we came close. Once again we were absorbed into another mêlée of immigration officials, customs, and armed police, with taxi drivers and porters hovering distantly, like predators in the background.

Nearly an hour was taken up with a further three lengthy recordings of our personal details in massive ledgers remarkably similar to those in use in Pakistan. I could understand why the earlier users of the Grand Trunk Road had decided to ignore the paperwork, and just fought their way in to India. Eventually we were through the hoops of the endless entry formalities. Perhaps we should have stuck to the tourist routes and flown in to Bombay or Delhi, and perhaps every other traveler had reached that conclusion, for there was no one of our kind seeking entry to India, or indeed to enter Pakistan, the way we went. We were alone. And clearly regarded as oddball, possibly suspicious, but probably harmless, even mentally deficient for electing to travel the way we were going. An hour later we were in Amritsar. We'd crossed the divide. Karachi was not only distant, but a far part of another world; and Lahore, sadly, seemed to have no more substance than an end stop on a road to nowhere. You could say that the very legitimacy of the city is now void, negated by the barbed wire of yet another border curtain.

Janet and Victoria both told me later they felt a sudden, extraordinary, and exhilarating freedom. Rather than being surrounded by furtive figures draped from head to foot in black burkhas, none of whom ever made eye contact, even with them, the change was revolutionary. For the first time they were greeted by smiling, welcoming females, unveiled, dressed in beautifully colored saris, whose only deference to a different custom was to join their palms together, incline the head, and say "Namaste." "Welcome." The millions of black-draped figures imprisoned inside those all-enveloping seventh-century robes are human beings too. The tragedy is that they may never feel the warmth of the morning sun on the backs of their necks, or an evening breeze ruffle their hair. They may never walk with their friends, laughing and joking down the streets, or ever stop at a coffee shop, having done their shopping.

❖   ◆   ❖

The border crossing we made is no longer possible. Why this enmity? I go back to the Partition of India in 1947. When the British realized that India must be granted independence, Muhammed Ali Jinnah, the leading Muslim politician, demanded the formation of a separate Muslim State. Mahatma Ghandi and Jawaharlal Nehru on the Hindu side were against it. India was secular, a land of many religions, and the population was inextricably mixed. In 1947 the British Government, washing its hands, appointed a new Governor, Lord Louis Mountbatten and set 1948 as the date for Independence.

A partition line was drawn up which split the Punjab, cutting the Grand Trunk Road between Lahore and Amritsar and, even worse, envisaged an East (Pakistan) and West (Bengal) Pakistan. Race riots were already common as the news of the coming division spread, and crazed desperate masses on both sides of the tenuous unmarked new frontiers were already trying to relocate themselves. Mountbatten, sensing chaos, possibly hoping to cut the lead-in period to settle the new nations down sooner rather than later, turned the heat up with a declaration that Independence Day was to be 14 August 1947. By that day more than eleven million people had lost their homes and became refugees; in rioting, chaos, and carnage half a million people lost their lives. The next year Ghandi was assassinated—not by a Muslim, but by a Hindu fanatic.

The frontiers drawn were untenable. Kashmir, a princely state with a Hindu ruler but a predominantly Muslim population, had been declared to be part of India. It remains a bone of contention to this day, divided on a "Cease Fire" line brokered by the United Nations at the outset, when both India and Pakistan were flying in troops to settle their dispute in war. Pakistan, as a matter of policy, ensured that its side of the line became the safe haven of Islamic militants, bent on forcing India to secede the entire state to Pakistan. Pakistan and India went to war in 1965, in the Punjab, which was a near defeat for Pakistan, and again in 1971. Pakistan once again came out worse, losing East Pakistan, which with Indian backing declared itself to be a new independent state: Bangladesh. The cost had been another three million lives.

It was a rare break that had allowed us to walk across the divide. The India we entered on foot had then, and still has, a considerable Muslim population. It outnumbers the entire population of Pakistan.

India

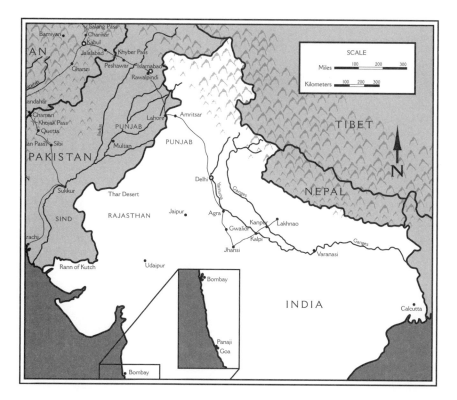

Five

A Dawn Communion

Welcome to India. It was bitterly cold in Amritsar, a reminder that it was still January and the highest mountain range in the world was not far to the north of us. We could find nowhere to eat that first night except one empty restaurant, the worst of all indicators, but by then any hot food was welcome, and the Kingfisher beer was cold. Our hotel was equally unpromising at first sight: no hot water, no light in the bathroom, and as we got into bed my foot went straight through a paper-thin top sheet. After losing points on our initial assessment, the hotel won gold stars by kicking in with a hot-air heating system that locked on, with no options, at full blast. A single, lonely, incongruous print was hanging opposite our bed, the only decoration on four bare walls, titled:

Snow in New York
Robert Henri 1865–1929
National Gallery of Art
Washington DC

Was it an antidote to the monsoon heat of an Indian summer? Or a reminder that we were lucky to have the fierce central heating?

Victoria and I woke in the morning all too conscious that we were still in the Punjab, the land of the five rivers, the land of winter temperature inversions. It was another river, but the same scene, like Lahore. The same morning white-out. Gray out? Scotch mist. Fog. Call it what you like, you couldn't see across the road. Janet hadn't moved when I got out of our bed. She lay enveloped in a cocoon of torn sheet and only the top of her head was visible. I sat beside her. A muffled voice said she had cholera. They had killed her. We could do what we wanted that morning. Just leave her alone.

Getting a bottle of Dioralyte was clearly on the to-do list, together with cashing traveler's checks to get rupees, and visiting the Indian Airlines office to book an afternoon flight to Delhi. There are times when you have to be prepared to write off a day for travel administration, simply to get to the next destination, and technically we were bound to move on without undue delay. Amritsar, lying in the Frontier Zone as it does, is closed to foreigners save those in transit. In the past it was a magnet for visitors, for it's the sacred city of the Sikhs, famed for its Golden Temple, the very heart of the Sikh religion, and I'd long wanted to go there. I had one other place on my visit list that morning. It was a park called the Jalianwala Bagh. It was there, in 1919, that a packed crowd of Indians attending a public meeting calling for independence from British rule had been gunned down in cold blood. Some four hundred were killed and twelve hundred wounded. The estimates were conservative. The numbers could well have been far higher. It was a murderous event of such horror that, having worn the uniform I'd worn for years, I felt a moral obligation to go there, in homage, a form of expiation necessary on three counts: national shame, human revulsion, and professional disgust at the events of 1919. I was in Amritsar. I could not turn my back and walk away.

We left Janet with a pack of Immodium and a bottle of mineral water. Victoria and I set out in a penetrating, invasive dampness to find a taxi. It was cold, about forty degrees Fahrenheit. We heard later that it was snowing to the north of us. We had an hour or so before banks and offices would open, so we headed for the Golden Temple. Within minutes we were wet, disoriented, and ready to turn back, but found an unhappy trishaw driver who, from his delight at seeing us, had clearly despaired of finding fares.

We hesitated when we reached the temple gateway. We were the only foreigners in sight and felt intrusive, quite apart from being chilled to the marrow, which can erode determination. The motivation to take off your shoes, wash your feet, and pad barefoot through the equivalent of a city block on a pavement of cold Jaipur marble was not high. We screwed up our resolve. Weak sunlight filtering through the blanket of stratus gave an illusion of tepid warmth. Mist was rising from the central water tank as we passed through the gateway under its clock tower and into the courtyard. The shrine of the Golden Temple, gray, ethereal, was in front of us, floating in air. We were soon befriended.

Hello. Were we English? American? Did we wish to see the Temple?

We hadn't presumed to approach the shrine. We were encouraged. We were made welcome. Ill-at-ease, not at all certain that we should be doing it, we joined the other pilgrims on the long causeway to the shrine on its apparent island, and there, like them, we received prasada, holy food, in our crossed palms. As we left the complex I noticed for the first time the bullet scars of the Indian Army assault on the temple in 1984, but neither of us spoke. You don't babble when you have the feeling that, in the stillness of a moment of frozen time, unexpectedly, you have stepped out of your own clothes. Evaluation of the experience has to be done slowly, and subliminally.

Some nineteen million people live in the Punjab, India's richest state. Sixty percent of the population is Sikh; the remainder is Hindu. Disenchantment with the Delhi Government led to Sikh demands for the establishment of an independent state, Khalistan, the land of the pure. Quite apart from the fate of the Hindu 40 percent of the Punjab population, a split of this magnitude, which would have been the third major fragmentation of Indian territory in forty years, might have brought about the end of India as a democracy, and as a nation.

The refusal of the government in Delhi to countenance this bid for secession led, as so often happens, to the formation of a terrorist movement dedicated to achieve its purpose through intimidation and murder. The occupation of the Golden Temple by Sikh terrorists, and its use by them as a stronghold, led Indira Ghandhi to order the army to storm the temple in 1984. It is easy to be wise after such events, but in retrospect the dilemma could have been better handled, politically and militarily. There had been no compelling political initiatives offered by the government. The Sikh's holiest shrine was defiled and over a thousand lives were lost in pursuit of a military objective. The terrorist movement was far from broken, inevitably retribution was sought in Hindu lives, and Mrs. Ghandhi herself was assassinated by her own, hitherto loyal, Sikh guards. In the rioting that followed her death, in Delhi and other cities, over four thousand Sikhs were killed.

In May 1988 Rajiv Ghandhi, the Prime Minister of India, faced an identical situation. His handling of the new crisis could not have been better. He had the Golden Temple surrounded by Special Forces, turned off the water supply and electricity, and waited. Any terrorist seen was shot, but no attempt was made to storm the sanctuary. After a week the siege produced results. A hundred terrorists surrendered, then more, and then the last fanatics came out with their hands up. Three had committed suicide.

If you want to accelerate yourself out of introspection back into day-to-day Indian life, try cashing a traveler's check at a bank. Try handling the knock-on effect of discovering that all Indian Airline flights have been cancelled, and no re-start date was known. The check cashing took the best part of an hour, and was an object reminder of the mind-blowing pedantry of Indian administration, be it in government or commerce. As for Indian Airlines, we were assured that no one was likely to fly out of Amritsar for four days. It hardly seemed an issue of concern in the ticket office. One day there would be flights. Not today. Or tomorrow. Maybe if we came back next Monday? It was Thursday. Victoria's time in India was running short. I wanted her to see Agra and Fatehpur Sikri. There was a train to Delhi at noon that day.

We left the Indian Airlines office to find a pharmacy, and inside a chaotic shop that was more like a bazaar than a clinical oasis of ordered counters, we found just about every drug, herb, and restorative known to western, eastern, and holistic medicine. Dioralyte was there. We had just enough time to go to the Jalianwala Bagh. Rather like entering the Golden Temple, I was not entirely certain that I wanted to go there, nor convinced that it was politic that we should. Somehow our stopover in Amritsar had become a heavyweight call, but I'd half expected that it would be this way, and I would not have moved on without making this second pilgrimage.

In 1918, to their dismay, the old European powers became aware that much of the colonial world had become infected by a new and tiresome spirit of nationalism. Of the fifty thousand soldiers of the British Indian Army who had fought in Europe, those who came back to their homeland were returning with their eyes open. The 1914–18 Great War had been a singularly bloody, senseless conflict, and it had had absolutely nothing to do with India. The nascent Indian independence movement, so hesitantly nurtured with the formation of the Indian National Congress in 1885, bogged down in its own rhetoric, had lost both a sense of direction and motive power. Catalysts came in two totally unexpected ways. The first was the return of Mohandas Karamchand Ghandi from British South Africa in 1915. He had made a name for himself there as a young lawyer looking after the rights of Indians, which, inevitably, had brought him into conflict with the colonial authorities. Ghandi's return might well have been enough by itself to turn the heat up, but the move for independence received a second, less pacific, activator: the devastating impact of 1,650 rounds of .303 rifle ammunition.

Conscious of the writing on the wall, in 1919 the British Government approved legislation, which, for the first time, gave Indians a say in the government of their own country. In proposing the act, the Secretary of State for India said the aim of the government was "the gradual development of self-governing institutions with a view to the progressive realization of responsible government in India as an *integral part of the British Empire."* The italics highlighting those last six words are mine. The proposals were too guarded, too grudging, and too slow. Ghandhi, convinced that non-violent protest would prove the most potent way to bring about independence, organized a series of hartals, one-day strikes and shop closures. The government over-reacted. A series of emergency measures were rushed into law before the new reforms had seen the light of day. Internment without trial was authorized, judges were given the power to try political cases without juries, the accused were not allowed legal representation, and there was no right of appeal against a sentence. Once the downslide had started, it went from bad to worse.

Ghandi was arrested. In Amritsar a crowd formed in a non-violent protest at further arrests. In a panicked, precipitous reaction to a protest march, ten Indians were killed, shot by British troops. Reactive rioting started. Brigadier-General Reginald Edward Harry Dyer arrived in Amritsar to take personal command of a mixed force of soldiers with no local sensitivities: Gurkhas (recruited from Nepal) and Baluchis (recruited from Quetta). Martial law was invoked. All processions and gatherings were banned, the meeting of more than four persons was declared an illegal assembly, and a curfew was imposed each night. These regulations were never publicized.

Sunday, April 13, was Baisakhi Day, a Sikh religious holiday, and the date of an annual cattle fair. Each year these events attracted a large number of peasants from outlying villages. The evening before, to take advantage of the holiday, plans had already been made to hold a public meeting in the Jalianwala Bagh, an enclosed open space within the eastern part of Amritsar, on Sunday afternoon.

On Sunday Dyer was told of the gathering. Supported by two armored cars, he marched straight to the Bagh. No one knows how many people were there when he arrived. Dyer's estimate was six thousand. There were more than that. Perhaps as many as twenty thousand people were crammed into the area, which is hardly an open space in the sense of an open garden or park. The Jalianwala Bagh is the basin of an old, vast water tank, its floor some four feet lower than the surrounding ground level, its sides still steep, and its periphery contained by the sides and backs of the houses around it. The ways into the open space were few, no more than four or five, all narrow slit passageways. Dyer couldn't get his armored cars into the area so he left them outside and marched fifty Gurkha riflemen through one of the passageways to the edge of the rim. There, under his command, they opened fire on the crowd without warning. For about ten minutes Dyer directed their fire, switching it from one part of the crowd to another, until their ammunition was almost exhausted. Dyer marched his soldiers out, back the way they had entered. The dead, the dying, and the wounded were left unattended. No attempt was made to summon help or make arrangements for their treatment.

The end result was whitewash, soft pedalling, and racial polarization. An eight-man committtee of inquiry, which included three Indians, produced, predictably, a Majority Report and a Minority Report. Despite the absolving weasel-wording of the majority finding, Dyer was retired on half-pay to a storm of protest in Britain. The House of Lords voted 129 to 86 against his unfair treatment, and a public subscription fund raised over twenty-six thousand pounds for "The Man Who Saved India." He should have been charged with murder.

In India Ghandhi swore never to wear European dress again, and declared that "cooperation in any shape or form with this satanic government is sinful." In 1920 he led the first of three nationwide campaigns of protest, which, eventually, forced the certainty of Indian independence.

The Jalianwala Bagh is a sad, sad place. The narrow entrance used by Dyer, a brick bund over an open drain, barely wide enough to let two men pass, remains unchanged. The position he took as his firing point is now a colonnaded terrace facing a memorial flame, but these changes apart, the area is as it was. You can appreciate the utter helplessness of those trapped there. The backs of the buildings, still pockmarked by bullets, hem you in, and the narrow approaches offer no escape. More than 120 people jumped into a well trying to save their lives. We walked around with a Sikh, his ten-year-old daughter, a younger son, and his nephew. There was no one else there at that time, and together we read the inscription, which began with these words:

THIS PLACE IS SATURATED WITH THE BLOOD OF ABOUT TWO THOUSAND HINDU, SIKH, AND MUSLIM PATRIOTS WHO WERE MARTYRED IN A NON-VIOLENT STRUGGLE TO FREE INDIA FROM BRITISH DOMINATION . . .

We had to race to the railway station and made it just in time for our train. The crowded streets, like those of any Indian city or town, offered a delight of advertising imagery and encouragement. LOOK AT ME BUT WITH LOVE was blazed on the tailgate of a garishly painted truck. The advertisements of Dr Rajiv, who was a SPECIALIST IN SEX AND LOVE, were uncompromising, but offered the promise of the entire Karma Sutra. More mundane were the fast-food temptations: HOLESOME SOUP, SANDWITCHES, and even a CICUEN SANDWITCH. Getting our tickets to Delhi, for we had no prior reservations, clearly presented unusual problems for the railway administration. Yes, there was a train to Delhi at noon. Yes, it had a First Class. We could buy tickets. But we had to make reservations first. Why? That was a silly question. That was the way it was done. So we paid eighteen rupees as a reservation fee, and were then allowed to buy our tickets. In return we were told that we could now travel on the train as we had reservations. We boarded and found the First Class carriage half empty.

It's a nine-hour journey from Amritsar to Delhi, and you learn a lot about Hindustan by going that way. If you fly you'll never realize the flatness and the immensity of the land, and you'll never have the cartoon shape of Indian palm trees, their feather duster tops capping their straight tall trunks like pom poms, printed in your memory. You'll miss the eucalyptus trees, and you'll miss being surprised at the extent to which this pinch-hit substitute for devastated native timber stands is taking over the countryside. You'll miss seeing rice paddy and water buffalo in a land where, most likely, you never expected to see the flora and fauna of the Far East. You can see all of this travelling by car, but few travel that way, for the car is not yet the mode of long-distance travel in India.

A car has one advantage over the train. If you go by train, you must anticipate the journey and, as far as you are able, ensure that you will never need to use the toilet. Such a need can, and will, spoil your journey, and western veterans of Indian travel fast before a train journey and fast during it. Janet, conditioned by Immodium, was in good shape. Somehow we survived this trial. Our nine hours went easily. By the third hour of the train journey we were sharing our fellow passengers's samosas and offering our own hastily bought, pathetic and less enterprising picnic fare in return. Six hours later we were in Delhi.

After brushing against cold reality during our Amritsar visits that morning, I did not tell Janet and Victoria, nor did I want to dwell on the fact that the rail route we had traveled, between Pakistan and the heartland of Northern India, had been the bloodiest pathway of the consequences of Partition in 1947. Trainload after trainload of refugees, desperately fleeing one country for the other, was attacked and everyone on board was killed. This mindless slaughter had formed the major part of the half-million death toll due to the Partition of British India.

Six

The Golden Triangle

The Golden Triangle—Delhi, Jaipur, and Agra—is the epicenter of tourism in India. Delhi features for it is the capital of the nation, and it has the provenance of a long history. Necessarily most tourists start there, but few stay long. List every potential negative in an evaluation of urban living, and Delhi has checkmarks in every box. This said, with just a week and half of Victoria's time in India to run, Delhi had to be taken at a run. In truth, as so little remains of the earlier cities, a one-night stay, maybe two at the most, satisfies most visitors. For us, Agra and the Taj Mahal were the obvious target in the Golden Triangle, for who would go to India, be within reach of the world's most famous memorial, and not see it? Even if you have to share the sight, shoulder to shoulder, with countless others? My own personal dream was to show Victoria Fatehpur Sikri, Akbar's abandoned city outside of Agra, at dawn. When no one else would be there.

"Ride with the tide." I told her "This circuit is the most heavily traveled tourist track in India. Keep cool, and we'll find some magic in it." By then we were on our way to the Red Fort.

No city I know, with a lifeline measured in centuries if not thousands of years, has not had a roller coaster ride, and left a raft of footprints. Delhi is no exception. Count seven, or is it eight cities there, of which two co-exist today. One is the overcrowded unplanned sprawl engulfing the plundered ruins of the Moghul Empire. That is Old Delhi. The other is a barren stage set built for its successor, the British Raj. That is New Delhi. It was in the Red Fort of Old Delhi, the walled city, that the feeble, toothless, eighty-two-year-old Bahadur Shah II, the last of the Moghul Emperors, was living when the firestorm of the Indian Mutiny broke out in 1857. The insurrection spread across Northern India. Delhi fell to the rebels in May that year. Four months later Delhi was recaptured by the British at a high cost in lives, no prisoners were taken, and an orgy of reprisal killings and looting went on until well into 1858. Bahadur Shah and his three sons were found hiding in the tomb of his ancestor, Humayon, five miles to the south of the Red Fort. His sons were stripped and summarily executed. Bahadur Shah was taken prisoner, tried for treason, convicted, and exiled to Rangoon, where he died four years later. It was the end of the Moghul line.

The Red Fort was plundered. The gemstones in the mosaics in the Diwan i Am, the Hall of Public Audiences and in the Diwan i Khas, the Hall of Private Audiences, had been prized from the walls with the points of bayonets. The masonry of the Red Fort was used as a source of building materials for barracks for the new British Indian Army, for clearly Delhi had to be garrisoned in future. As for the great public rooms and private apartments in the palace complex, nothing was worth preserving. Nothing was restored. The famous couplet on the walls of the empty Diwan i Khas

**If paradise on earth there be
'Tis here, 'tis here, 'tis here!**

could be taken, given the sorry state of the place, as the epitaph of Moghul India.

To complete the punishment and isolation of Delhi, and the severance of all that Delhi was believed to stand for in Indian minds, the capital of British India was established in Calcutta. None the less, some subliminal feeling of guilt about the fate of Delhi must have existed in London. In 1876 when Benjamin Disraeli persuaded Queen Victoria that she should set the seal on British supremacy by taking the title of Kaisar-i-Hind, Empress of India, the news was not announced in Calcutta but proclaimed, with deliberate pomp and ceremony, at a durbar (a state occasion akin to a coronation) in Delhi.

As we padded dutifully around the Red Fort that morning, where Janet and I had been each time we'd stayed in Delhi, we soon realized that the third member of our tour group was not greatly taken by what we had to offer as guides. After the Fort, other than the Jamid Masjid, the great mosque, and the Raj Ghat on the bank of the Yamuna, where Ghandi was cremated, that was it for Old Delhi. We took a taxi to New Delhi to complete the tourist round, and then turned our attention to the perennial preoccupation of travel: how best to get to the next destination? There was, that day, a not unusual near-manic desperation in our need to move on. Delhi was suffering from a pollution-induced washout that made the whole city appear like a faded sepia print. The atmosphere was insufferable. The *National Herald* forecast disaster. Merely breathing Delhi air, they said, was the equivalent of smoking thirty cigarettes a day. The grim report was underpinned with statistics. Within the area of the old once-walled city alone there were 868 pollution-producing industrial plants. Records, started in 1982, showed there had been a fifty-five percent increase in airborne pollutants. If nothing else, the broad, open streets of New Delhi might, momentarily, give the illusion of clean air. We went to Connaught Place, the business center, to attend to our travel. The first step was to go to the main Indian Airlines office and get flights to Agra.

Delhi–Agra is a high density route with frequent flights. We thought there would be no problems. At 1:45 pm fifty-eight people were waiting in the Indian Airlines office. The counters, curiously, were unmanned. Deserted. Twenty minutes later a clerk came out, looked startled to see some seventy people waiting, and started to give out slips: pink if you wanted to buy a ticket, green if you wanted to confirm a reservation. The next twenty minutes passed in an upheaval of organization. An hour passed. It was patently obvious that the pink-green system was failing, the waiting crowd had increased to mob proportions, and by then the frightened distributor of tickets had been joined by four others, facing forty-three angry people at the counter (I counted heads), with another forty-eight in the second row. A French couple behind me, already showing signs of wear, threw in the towel.

The first word was an expletive. "Pourquoi faire simple, quand on peut faire compliqué?" They quit at that point.

A new friend, born of the line-up, turned to me and asked where I was going.

"We're trying to get to Agra."

"Then I do not know why you are booking this flight."

"Why is that?"

"Because, I am knowing this, there are no seats until February." It was January 8. We inched forward in the line. Somehow, possibly by not resorting to brute force, we got our tickets. The business of the day completed, we could return to sightseeing.

It was in 1911 that a star architectural team, Sir Edwin Lutyens and Sir Herbert Baker, received a brief to build a new Delhi, a capital fit for the British Raj. The task was to take twenty-nine thousand men eighteen years to achieve at a cost of £10 million; and the Viceroy's House, or so it was disingenuously named, took its final form as a 340-room palace. New Delhi is a classic example of imperial megalomania. The ultimate failure of the grand plan lay in simple trigonometry. The Viceroy's House, now the President's Residence, was intended to stand proud, like an Indian Versailles, at the end of the Raj Path, the great central ceremonial road. It is invisible. Below the horizon. Go to the far end, the India Gate, and look. As for the Parliament Buildings, it's personal taste I know, but to my mind the complex looks like a federal penitentiary. If nothing else, they got the width of the streets right. Part of the instructions given to Lutyens and Baker were that the street plan for the capital should facilitate riot control and the suppression of insurrections. The streets, like the avenues of Paris, were to allow the deployment cannon, and in this case, armored cars. The urban battle plan brought one dividend. Today, in New Delhi, traffic can move. In Old Delhi it moves at a crawl, that is if it moves at all. In the 1930s, when the whole extravagance of the new capital was deemed complete, it appeared that the British were there to stay. Had Amritsar in 1919 been forgotten?

By the turn of the century the British Empire was at its zenith. The endless colonial wars and campaigns of Victoria's reign were over, and the Union Jack flew unchallenged in every band of latitude. For the privileged few, the upper and middle classes of what Lord Lugard called "the greatest governing race the world has ever seen," it was a time of unprecedented peace, prosperity, and supreme self-confidence. The death of Victoria in 1901 and the accession of Edward VII, who due to his mother's longevity had no more than nine years of his own life to run, heralded the start of this new era. In 1905 the Prince and Princess of Wales toured India, an imperial progression that might have made the great Akbar think twice about status symbols. The seed had been sown for a fantastic display of British power, which was to prove the climax of the British Raj when they, in turn, became King George V and Queen Mary.

A return visit would be the first time that a reigning British monarch had visited India. It was set in train. A Coronation Durbar would be held in Delhi in December 1911, and there the whole of India would pay homage to their Imperial Majesties in person. At its climax the King would announce that the capital of India was to be moved back to its ancient site, a decision that had been kept a secret from the general public, and, inexplicably, from Queen Mary. For ten days Delhi might have been described as an endlessly rolling triumphal march from Aida in an Indian setting, but the opera pales in comparison. There were State Entries and flourishes of trumpets, 101-gun salutes, and the act of homage by the princes and ruling chiefs of Hyderabad, Baroda, Mysore, Kashmir, Rajputana, Central India, Baluchistan, Sikkim, Bhutan, the United Provinces, the Punjab, Bengal, Assam, and the North West Frontier; and then Madras and Bombay paid court to the Crown, and Burma was brought in to join in the genuflection. Every step in the brilliantly choreographed, rehearsed, and stage-managed display went exactly as had been intended:

> **"the King-Emperor and Queen-Empress will move in procession from the Durbar Shamiana to the Royal Pavilion. They will advance hand in hand, their Robes being held by Pages and golden Umbrellas held over their heads . . ."**

My quote comes from what, today, I guess we'd call the screenplay. It is the handbook governing the entire event, which I have to hand, for my grandfather was Military Secretary to the Commander-in-Chief in India at that time, and I have his copy of it.

A special camp was built for the occasion northwest of Delhi Ridge. It was the same site that had been chosen in 1877 by Lord Lytton, then Viceroy, to make public Queen Victoria's adoption of imperial status, and Lord Curzon, dramatic and stagey, had used the same place for his 1903 Durbar. But now it was the real thing. Two amphitheaters were built, one with twelve thousand seats reserved for Governors, the Commander-in-Chief, Lieutenant Governors, and other high officials, together with the ruling chiefs, Durbaris from British India and the Native States, as well as guests of the government and other privileged spectators. The other amphitheater, seating fifty thousand, was given over to the general public. The Durbar ceremony itself was just the focal point in a series of royal events, which included a reception for the ruling chiefs, the unveiling of a memorial to King Edward, a military church parade, a State Reception, the Presentation of Colours to eight British and two Indian battalions, a State Garden Party, a military Review, an Investiture, and a Review of the Police. There were polo matches, hockey and football finals, boxing tournaments, tent pegging competitions (riding at a full gallop to spear a line of wooden tent pegs with a lance), Point to Point races, native sports, and a Badshahi Mela or People's Fête.

Such an extravaganza required a strong supporting cast. Twenty thousand troops and forty-eight military bands were brought to Delhi and their needs and well being required the kind of stage management not seen since Akbar built Fatepur Sikri. Special railways were constructed, both broad and narrow gauge, together with new rail stations and over one hundred miles of new roads. A 2,400-kilowatt coal-burning generating station was built, which consumed three thousand tons of coal in the Durbar period alone. Ten thousand lighting poles were erected together with nine hundred miles of power lines, 101 miles of water pipeline were laid, and five million gallons of water a day were pumped into the camp area. Twenty-four post offices were built and opened. A central market was set up (for wines, spirits, oilman's stores, tobacco, tailoring, saddlery, and chemist's supplies) together with a market for the sale of fruits, vegetables, flowers, bread, cakes, biscuits, jams, jellies, flour, rice, and grains. A third market catered for the sale of beef, mutton, poultry, eggs, fish, and game. And there was a dairy with a dedicated herd of two thousand milch cattle looked after by "four hundred dairymen and sixty Europeans". I use the description of the day. I end my statistics, in the light of the dairy, on an agricultural note. The whole set-up, cows and cavalry horses, required the importation of well over ten thousand tons of animal feed, for the most part hay, and nearly a thousand tons of baled bedding grass. The quarter-masters were kept busy. The end result was a stupendous and highly visible demonstration of British authority in India. It cost a fortune to lay on; but this hardly mattered, for the purse of India was deep, and India paid.

Nothing like it would be held again, for in 1914 the world of crowned heads, grand titles, empires, and sovereignty "by grace of God" took a shock from which it never recovered. There were state occasions yet to be played out, but by then it was no more than ritualized play acting, make-believe— but was not Delhi in 1911 in this category of costume drama too?

On an earlier visit to Delhi I'd had a tough time finding the site of the Coronation Durbar. My 1911 map had been overtaken by some seventy-five years, and a Delhi city map was little help. It was, I knew, well to the north of the walled city and in the end I navigated by the more enduring features, the run of the Yamuna River and the nullahs, the water channels and irrigation canals. Suddenly I picked up a sign that read KINGSWAY CAMP, and I knew I was close, but there was nothing there: just a desolation of wasteland, camel thorn, and bare dirt. Then a circular section of old road became evident, and soon after I discovered that I was in a half circle of crumbling red sandstone statue bases. In the center there was an obelisk with a lengthy inscription on a plaque:

HERE ON THE 12TH DAY OF DECEMBER 1911
HIS IMPERIAL MAJESTY KING GEORGE V
EMPEROR OF INDIA
ACCOMPANIED BY THE QUEEN EMPRESS
IN SOLEMN DURBAR
ANNOUNCED IN PERSON TO THE GOVERNORS
PRINCES AND PEOPLES OF INDIA
HIS CORONATION CELEBRATED IN ENGLAND
ON THE 22ND DAY OF JUNE 1911
AND RECEIVED FROM THEM
THEIR DUTIFUL HOMAGE AND ALLEGIANCE

I walked on through the scrub towards a colossal white statue half visible through the thorn trees. The browsing goats eyed me warily as I walked into the area that had been the second amphitheater to find a mega-statue of the crowned King Emperor, in robes that fell twice the height of the man down a pedestal that dwarfed anyone standing at its base. The King Emperor was faced by two flanking half-circles of statues, former

Governors perhaps; many were missing. Everything was desolation. Ruin. Litter and thorn scrub. I would give no prizes to anyone who thought of Shelley's Ozymandias, for if ever there was a final comment to be written about the Coronation Durbar, his lines are it:

> I met a traveller from an antique land
> Who said: Two vast and trunkless legs of stone
> Stand in the desert. Near them, on the sand,
> Half sunk, a shattered visage lies, whose frown,
> And wrinkled lip, and sneer of cold command
> Tell that its sculptor well those passions read
> Which yet survive, stamped on these lifeless things—
> The hand that mocked them and the heart that fed;
> And on the pedestal these words appear:
> "My name is Ozymandias, king of kings:
> Look on my works, ye Mighty, and despair!"
> Nothing beside remains. Round the decay
> Of that colossal wreck, boundless and bare
> The lone and level sands stretch far away.

The Moghul succession had ended in 1858. Despite the greatest stage show ever mounted, British rule came to an end in 1947. Eighty-nine years was perhaps the shortest run in recorded history for imperial domination on this scale, but it left India changed forever.

Landing in Agra we taxied past Indian Air Force fighter bombers parked in a combat-ready dispersal pattern on the apron, past a wrecked World War II aircraft, the buildings of the Indian Army Parachute School, and a lot of barbed wire. It was, I thought, a bizarre approach to a Moghul city. Somehow in the milling crowd outside the terminal we found a taxi. Our journey to the center of the town took almost as long as it had taken to fly from Delhi. The traffic was what you could call "Indian standard," chaotic, near gridlock, but perhaps our snail-like progress was fortunate, for sitting in front I got to know our driver, Jagdishparshad. We talked happily of

Moghul Emperors and the mixed blessings of tourism, and with Jag at my elbow I took advantage of one interminable traffic jam to buy a bottle of "Romanov Extra Smooth Vodka" in the bazaar for 120 rupees. I expected an ovation for opportunism. To my dismay my trophy with its patently untrue label, questionable origin, place of purchase, and $8 price tag, clearly aroused deep suspicion and grave reservations from my jury in the back seat.

We were staying at the Mughal Sheraton. It was my treat for my uncomplaining companions, who had been living a touch distanced from any form of luxe, let alone grand luxe. I'm not certain that it's wise, after twelve days of independent travel, to plunge so suddenly back into one of the epicenters of the tourist world. Five tour buses, engines running, were blocking the hotel driveway, and the hotel entrance was inaccessible, sealed off by a mountain of suitcases. Trapped in hot sun between these barriers, thirty elderly tourists were making a last-ditch stand against the insistent solicitation of a mahoot with a dusty elephant; someone with a gaudily caparisoned bad-tempered camel; a snake charmer with his mongoose and two baskets of cobras; some six or seven tour guides laden with brochures, guidebooks, and postcards; and a grossly overloaded carpet salesman, who was struggling to find display space. Faced with that reception party, Semiramis herself might have thought twice about staying in India.

We escaped to seek refuge inside the hotel lobby, only to find over two hundred people trying to check in at the same time. In the midst of this chaos an aging night club princess with long, dyed, blonde hair was posing for "Arrival in Agra" shots for her point-and-shoot camera–wielding overweight geriatric boyfriend. She had clearly spent some time getting her outfit right: in-style dark glasses, a shirt unbuttoned to within two inches of her navel, a mini skirt, silver nautch girl anklets festooned with little bells, and black high heels. Jag left us in this nightmare, but not before I'd hired him for two days. There was, I could tell, no point in fooling around. We needed him.

We dined at the hotel that evening, and I had a post-dinner plan. In the days when I was running the Wilderness Foundation UK for Laurens van der Post, a not-for-profit organization devoted to conservation promotion and education, we'd started by offering foot safaris in Kenya. Once they were going, we'd talked of expanding and setting up a program in India.

The one drawback, as I saw it, was that no one would be prepared, however interested they might be in wildlife, to travel to India and return, never having seen the Taj Mahal and some of the other fabled, famous tourist destinations. To obviate this potential pitfall, I'd set up a tour I named Wildlife and Palaces. We combined Delhi, Jaipur, and Agra with three national parks: Corbett, in the foothills of the Himalayas; Sariska in Western Rajasthan; and Bharatpur, not far from Agra. We ran one tour monthly in season, October to April. I'd worked it so that our clients arrived in Agra in the early evening of a full moon night. They settled in their hotel, and had dinner. Then we took them to the Taj Mahal, having never disclosed the reason for our timing. The word must have spread. About two years later, after I'd left the Wilderness Foundation, I was idly browsing through a batch of tour leaflets on India. Just about everyone in the trade was offering park and palace combinations, and more than one talked of the Taj Mahal by moonlight.

This visit my timing was off by two or three days. The moon was almost full, and half the world was there. I'd expected it, for in the eight- day period bracketing a full moon the Taj stays open until midnight. The five tour buses had been waiting outside the hotel that evening, and were there, at the entry gate. But even with the crowd scene, if you stand back, you find that the sheer size of the Taj Mahal and its surrounding park reduces its visitors to insignificance. Does it match your expectations? The answer is "yes." It's magic seen at a distance, ethereal seen in moonlight, stunning in its impact by day, far larger close-to than you would, somehow, have believed. At arm's length a measure of sadness creeps in, when you see the effects of atmospheric pollution.

The next morning we were on the road before dawn, heading for Fatehpur Sikri. In the villages cooking fires were being fanned to life, the first women were going to the wells, and flocks of peacocks were feeding in the still dark fields. As the light strengthened with the red of the rising fireball behind us we saw pairs of sarus crane; it's almost always pairs for they mate for life. We saw black ibis and rose ringed parakeets, and there were parrots on the entry gate to the city when we arrived. We had Akbar's almost perfectly preserved abandoned capital to ourselves for nearly an hour. We made our way slowly through the site and the shadows of night were erased as the sun rose, as if floodlights were being switched on as we went from building to building. When we left the tour buses were grinding in, and the dancing bears, the pathetic standard offering on the Agra-

Fatehpur Sikri road, were out in force. Back in Agra traffic had gridlocked. We tried the Red Fort. It was a nightmare at the high tide of the tourist day. We fled to Itimad-Ud-Daula and to our surprise, no one else was there.

The Fatehpur Sikri of my dawn delight was the capital planned and built by Akbar, the rebuilder of Lahore, in 1569. Twenty-three miles west of Agra, an outlying ridge of the Vindhya Hills dominates the village of Sikri and the surrounding countryside. It was this ridgeline that Akbar selected as his green field site. The Fatehpur in its title means "City of Victory" to commemorate a victory won four years after construction had started. Eighteen years later Fatehpur Sikri was abandoned. The generally accepted reason for a precipitate departure from a mini-city, which, by any standards, was close to perfection, is that the local water supply failed. Akbar's city was left untouched, never pillaged for its stone, and has remained perfectly preserved on its commanding ridgeline, and the surrounding countryside, far from the near-desert you might expect, is green with crops.

Akbar's design is brilliant, the architecture is world class, and its red sandstone (some of which Akbar himself was said to have helped quarry and carve) is stunning. All this is the tangible, highly visual side. Less apparent are the traces of Akbar's multi-racial tolerance, in which his own credo admitted Hindu, Buddhist, and Christian beliefs, together with his own faith in Islam. The quotation carved in the portal of the great 154-foot-tall Gate of Victory, the Buland Darwaza, puts it in three sentences:

> **Said Jesus, on whom be peace: the world is but a bridge; pass over but build no houses on it. He who hopes for an hour, hopes for Eternity, for the world is but an hour. Spend it in devotion, for the rest is unseen.**

Agra Fort, which we had failed to re-visit, is another Akbar construction project, later much modified and turned from fortress into palace. Akbar's grandson, Shah Jehan, was imprisoned there by his son, Aurangzeb, for the last seven years of his life. He was said to have spent most of his time in the Octagonal Tower, which he had built, looking out at his greatest architectural triumph, the tomb he had planned and constructed for his beloved Mumtaz, his greatly-loved, favorite wife. The Taj Mahal, from there, seems almost within reach, just further along the same bank of the Yamuna river.

Itimad-Ud-Daula is on the other side of the Yamuna. It's the tomb built by Mumtaz Mahal's mother for her father, who was the Emperor Jahangir's (Akbar's son) chief minister. The draw is that this tomb, placed in the center of an early Moghul garden, is the pocket-sized forerunner of the Taj Mahal.

❖   ◆   ❖

Over our next day and half in Agra a new dimension came into our lives. It was "load shedding," relieving overtaxed power plants by cutting the supply of electricity at source. We had five shutdowns, and getting by with flickering candles in the Moghul Sheraton made it seem as if we were taking part in some surrealistic experiment in living. We should have anticipated the inevitable on our last morning. There was a weather clampdown, meaning no flights in or out of Agra. Victoria and Janet were due to fly back to London from Karachi within thirty-six hours.

We raced to Agra Cantonment railway station to take the Shatabdi Express to Delhi. A "load shed" plunged the station into primeval gloom while we waited for the train to arrive, long after its advertised departure time. At last, after the normal tooth and claw fight to board an Indian train, we were there, seated on one of India's premier trains, all airline reclining seats, faded floral pink curtains hung under raspberry pink pelmets, and a blue carpet that looked as if it had never been cleaned. The overall decor might have looked better under anything but fluorescent lights. There were occasional random bursts of music over the loudspeakers, and then the audio system mercifully failed. A meal was served, airline style in plastic trays, a chicken curry still on the bone, which required some skill to handle with nothing but a plastic spoon. All the while a woman with a sleeping baby in her arms walked up and down the aisle, manifestly in the way of the attendants handing out and collecting trays, but she remained hell-bent on her promenading. It was neither comfortable nor relaxing, and the drab, hard-cushion simplicity of going First Class Amritsar to Delhi, in retrospect, seemed infinitely preferable.

We reached Delhi, spoilt western children maybe, regretting that we hadn't been able to fly. Surely the weather factor couldn't have been that bad? The following morning we learned that an Indian Air Force helicopter had taken off from Agra, the crew certain that they would have no problems with the weather. They crashed, somewhere near Gorakhpur, in dense fog. Two were killed and two survived, injured. I suddenly thought of the train derailment in the Sind Desert. A second escape? Thank God Indian Airlines had not flown. And so in Delhi, just before dawn the next morning, I said goodbye to Janet and Victoria. They were as assured as anyone on the Indian sub-continent could ever be of making their Karachi deadline by way of a direct flight to Bombay, but I felt traitorous deserting them, and breaking the bond of our group of three.

I took the Shatabdi Express back to Agra. I'd made a deal with Jag , our taxi driver, before we'd left that city. He would find a car, which I would rent, and he would drive, taking time off from his taxi driving. Together we'd set out into Central India, and sometime, whenever it might be, we'd bring the circle back to his home in Agra. Jag knew that I was bent on following the faint footprints of the Rani of Jhansi through the final, critical four months of her fight against the British in the Indian Mutiny of 1857–58, and with his help I might be able translate my histories, memoirs, and maps into some kind of reality. He was, I think, quite taken with the project. I'd asked him what he knew about the Rani of Jhansi and his reply was brief, but right on the button:

"Not very much, but she was very brave, I am thinking, and your people did not like her."

So at Agra Cantonment railway station the day before it had only remained to fix a start date.

"I'll take the first train from Delhi tomorrow, Jag, the one that leaves at six. Then we can get away from Agra early."

"I will be waiting for you."

As the train left Delhi I felt suddenly, shatteringly lonely. At that moment my motivation to desert my females, and turn away to cross Central India, chasing the fleeting shadow of a woman I would never meet, and could never meet, was close to zero. The paths you take in life can be deceptively casual, or so it seems in retrospect. Rarely are there significant road junctions, with signs, and warnings if they are needed, telling you what lies ahead. Why was I on the Shatabdi Express heading back to Agra, having abandoned Janet and Victoria, hell-bent on the pursuit of a singularly attractive, dynamic, and brave young Indian woman, who, as it happened, had died prematurely, and violently, seventy-seven years before my time? The responsibility lies entirely with the Cunard Line. Let me backtrack eight years.

Main Street, Quetta 1968.

Kashgar design Gardner bowl.

1

Gardner china mark (on a coffee cup).

The Towers of Victory at Ghanzi. Evening. Janet with Edward.

Spring snow-melt in the Hindu Kush. The Salang Pass.

The north end of the Salang Tunnel.

Tunnels under the citadel at Lashkargah (Qala Bist).

Lashkargah (Qala Bist) coins. The head of the Great King of Kings, Orthagenes. Minted at Alexandreia Arachoris (Kandahar) AD 35–55.

Horse head knife hilt from Lashkargah (Qala Bist).

A Kandahar stone cutter with Edward helping.

5

The flash flood that nearly took the car away on the Herat Road.

Victoria's hand decorated with henna for a Karachi wedding.

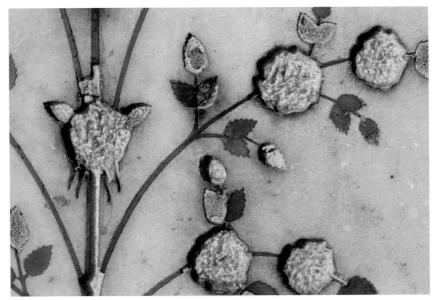

A marble panel in the Red Fort, Delhi, where gemstones were prised out by British bayonets.

Early morning outside the Victory Gate (Buland Darwaza) at Fatehpur Sikri.

Carved marble screens at Fatehpur Sikri.

Indian miniature portrait of the Rani of Jhansi c1856–57. National Army Museum, London.

Evening light on the Rani's temple in Jhansi Fort.

The smoke of the first funeral pyres at dawn in Varanasi.

Sunrise at Varanasi on the Ganges.

The temple at Satichaura Ghat in Kanpur.

Engraving of the 1857 Satichaura Ghat massacre.

The Maha Lakshmi temple at Jhansi and the old boatman.

Early photograph of Jhansi Fort c1859–60. National Army Museum, London.

The Yamuna River from the terrace in Kalpi.

The first entry gate to Gwalior Fort.

Undated early photograph of Gwalior Fort. National Army Museum, London.

The Portuguese cathedral in Vela (old) Goa.

A girl selling bangles and necklaces on a beach near Karmane, Goa.

Contrasts in living, Mumbai (Bombay).

The Lake Palace in Udaipur.

The interior of the Mother Temple at Nagada.

A rajah with a companion, possibly a nautch girl. Miniature painting on ivory in Moghul style. Bought in Udaipur 1968. Artist unknown.

Seven

Entr'acte. When Everything Became Red

The date was 1983. I was in the Cunard offices in Southampton. We were talking about *QE 2* lecture programmes. I'd been asked to lecture during the Indian Ocean sector of the next world cruise. I'd suggested talking about Kenya, for I'd spent time there, and it might turn to advantage for the Wilderness Foundation. To talk of India was out of the question. It was too vast a canvas, too complex, and outside my compass. What on earth would you choose as a subject? I must have asked the question aloud.

"Why don't you talk about the Mutiny? After all, you were a soldier, weren't you?"

I had serious reservations. Were lectures of murder, fire, blood, and revenge the right fare for a cruise ship? Wasn't the terrible saga of 1857 and 1858 better left alone now? Arguably those two fateful years had generated a greater weight of paper, books, diaries, and memoirs, measured in poundage of paper against calendar years, than any other conflict. Most of them, predictably, were highly partisan. What more was there to say?

I stalled, asked for time, and went back to talk with Janet.

After our year in Pakistan and Afghanistan, India was high on my travel list. It was partly to redress the balance. It was partly the draw of the two generations before me who had served in India. Even further back my great-great-great-great-great grandfather, Mathew Wilson, who was born in 1730, married Frances Clive, the sister of Robert Clive, the first Lord Clive of India. The date of their marriage was 1759, two years after Clive's victory at Plassey had secured the whole of Bengal for the British East India Company. For years after this Wilson girls were given Clive as one of their names, and the two families were linked. It's this kind of historical baggage that can prompt your decision making.

"I sometimes wonder they do not cut all our heads off and say nothing about it."

The writer was Emily Eden, the sister of Lord Auckland, Governor General of India during the period 1835–42, who lived and travelled with her brother during his years of office in India.

She was right on target. Fifteen years after the Edens left India, a widespread revolt broke out against the British. Essentially the prime cause was the unrelenting and apparently unarrestable pace of British expansion, as India was "taken over" piecemeal, state by state.

Fifteen years after the Edens left India half the land had been taken under British rule; a determined missionary effort threatened every aspect of traditional Indian life; and the arrival of European women had brought about the near total estrangement of the two races. This social foment was exacerbated by the celerity of change in British India, as new roads, railways, canals, and telegraph lines were laid out and pushed ahead regardless of land rights, regardless of the destruction of temples, villages, and houses. The surviving Indian states felt threatened as, one by one, native rulers were brought under British domination and lawful inheritance was set aside if it countered the interests of their new overlords. In effect the British were writing new laws as they expanded their territory by establishing garrisons, and appointing advisers to each princely court. One signal change, never ratified by the Indians themselves, was that they would accept only direct male line primogeniture as a valid succession. A succession to a collateral branch of the same family, or to an adopted child, was ruled invalid. This was not in accordance with Hindu or Islamic law, nor indeed with English law. If there was no heir under this ruling, the British took over the State. The garrisons were there to underwrite the change.

By 1856 the imminent crisis was apparent, to those who could see it. Chappattis were mysteriously passed by runner from village to village with the message "make five more like these and pass them on." There was widespread fear, for a verbal message "Everything will become Red" was passed on with the "chain letter" biscuits. What did the message mean? Was it the red of the British soldier's tunic, meaning that the whole of India would be taken over? Was it the red the British used to color their possessions on maps? Was it the red of fire? Was it the red of blood? In April 1857 the burnings started in the night. Barrack buildings, stores, and huts were set on fire.

The flare-up came and the insurrection was branded as mutiny, but it was more than that: it was a chaotic, unplanned reaction against total subjection under foreign domination. None the less, of course it was a mutiny. The British had used force every step of the way in their progress across India. The initial counteraction could only come from their own locally recruited levies, for they were armed and trained to fight. Peasant revolts, gallant and heartfelt though they may be, are invariably tragic, disastrous failures.

The virtually spontaneous uprisings of 1857 were a moment of national crisis, universally perceived, universally recognised, but it seems that amongst those who revolted against British rule, there was no one in India with the charisma and determination to turn such a tidal surge of events to advantage. It was a major watershed, the end of the old India, and it was to prove the end of the Moghul line. Akbar's India, Akbar's power, and the wealth of his court, which once supported a household of 1,000 elephants, 30,000 horses, 400 tame deer, and 800 concubines, was gone forever. The revolt lasted two years. It was bitterly fought with terrible atrocities on both sides: the Indians were desperate, and the re-conquering retribution of the British was quite inhuman. In general opinion it was, and is, held that the result was a foregone conclusion for two reasons. The first was that once the weight of the British Imperial war machine got rolling, nothing could stop it. The second was that no Indian leader was equal to the challenge of the day.

Both judgements are summary, and not absolutely true. There was one outstanding leader on the Indian side: a young woman. Lakshmibai, the Maharani of Jhansi, was the widow of an Indian prince. She was twenty-two years old when she became involved in the events of the Mutiny, and she was killed in action the next year. In 1858, as city after city was sacked and devastated in revenge for the mutiny, she held center stage in Central India for some four months in a last-ditch fight against the overriding weight of British arms. Her worst fears were realised when her own Jhansi was stormed, and the city was destroyed. Legend has it that in the final stage of the siege the young Rani tied her child, the boy Rajah, to her back, mounted her horse, and vaulted the fortress walls to fight on, and die in battle at Kotah-ki-Serai, outside Gwalior.

In contemporary British mutiny records she is vilified as the epitome of heathen evil. Damned out of hand for the part she played in 1857 and 1858, and doubled damned for her sex, which had her branded as wanton at best, nymphomaniac beyond a doubt. In my reading, reinforced as I found other sources, it became self-evident that she had been feared, possibly greatly feared, by her adversaries. It is not uncommon that those who are feared most are demonized. Her age was immaterial. Her achievements were brushed aside. Were you to cite the very antithesis to the sweetness, gentleness, and piety of Victorian womanhood, she was the unmentionable example.

It remains that at a critical point in the violent genesis of the British Raj out of the shattered fabric of Moghul India, a stunningly attractive young woman, barely out of her teens, who hardly had the strength to wield a sword, shot to meteoric stardom like a brief bright flame. She came close to altering the path of history; and, but for a secondary role dictated by her sex and the blind chauvinism of her less-intelligent and less-talented male peers, she might well have headed a new, reunited India.

❖ ◆ ❖

Having given my word that I would lecture on Cunard's 1984 *Queen Elizabeth 2* World Cruise, Janet and I went to India to bring my reading to life, and to take slides. We'd covered much of Northern India, following the course of events in 1857 and 1858, and then, in its turn, Jhansi came up on the radar. We drove from Lakhnao to Jhansi, and that afternoon I took Janet to the fort.

Unless you have become immersed in Indian history, I do not believe you would wish to visit Jhansi. Other than the fort, which dwarfs half the city, there is little to draw you there, and no place where you would wish to stay. In truth Jhansi rates sadly low on the proverbial 1–10 scale. If you stop there, for it's on the road from Agra to Khajuraho, you'll find a statue of the Rani, caught in the moment of her escape. The sculptor has served her well, reins in one hand, sword in the other, a rearing horse, the boy Rajah tied behind her. The same dramatic "photo-op" freeze is repeated in statues of her in Gwalior, and in Hamipur. There's little more to see in Jhansi city.

If you have time, climb up to the Fort. It dominates Jhansi. Once on the walls you realise how close to being impregnable it was, although there's one low point on the walls where the hillside rides high. This is the place where legend has it that the Rani vaulted the wall at full gallop with her small boy, and broke through the enemy lines to escape. Weak spot that it is, Jhansi Fort was never taken in battle; but what was the point in continuing to fight there when your people were being slaughtered under your walls? As you walk through the Fort, climbing always to higher levels, much of it is abandonment, dereliction. There is evidence of later British occupation; but nothing of the Rani, other than the graves of her defenders, one of them her female gunner, Moti Bai. Janet and I were alone there, wandering wherever our curiosity took us, and then our freedom to wander was challenged by a troop of rhesus monkeys, led by a big old male who advanced screaming with bared teeth. I picked up stones to throw at him in case he came closer. We detoured around the pack, and then we no longer threatened their territory.

Further into the Fort we found an inner courtyard, which had been a garden at one time. It was a desolation. Lakshmibai's quarters, now in ruins, had their access from this garden courtyard, and from her windows she could look out over her beloved Jhansi. One further courtyard you can only access from her garden has a small Hindu temple shielded under the trees. Far from abandoned, it was still tended. A priest came out and as we made namaste, he greeted us in turn. He made no move to invite us to enter, so we stayed outside, said farewell, and retraced our steps.

I went back to the Fort alone that evening, leaving Janet in the Government Guest House where we were staying that night. I walked up the entry ramp and around the ramparts, and then crossed the central courtyard. The troop of monkeys was still there, still sensitive and still as aggressive when they felt their territory was threatened. I gave them a wide berth, not ready to take them on, and passed into the private sector of the Fort. For nearly an hour I stayed in the last light of the sun in the wilderness of the courtyard outside her apartments, the place that had been her garden. There was no one else there. The grass was knee deep and cascades of red roses tumbled from the battlements, and climbed, brier on brier, to form tangled thickets of jungle where once there had been rose beds.

> I sometimes think that never blows so red
> The Rose as where some buried Caesar bled
> That every Hyacinth the Garden wears
> Dropt in her Lap from some once Lovely Head.

It was corny and obvious to think of the Omar Khayyám quatrain, but it fitted. I walked through the great gateway to the outer courtyard where the small temple sits dwarfed by the massive encircling walls. The temple seemed larger than it had appeared that afternoon, but it was a trick of the hour, the inclination of the sun. The single simple white dome of the Hindu chapel was amber in the evening light. I took my shoes off, and entered. The priest showed no surprise. It was as if he had been waiting for me. He had no English. I had no fluent Hindi, only phrasebook single words or one-liners. The apparent communication barrier of our afternoon visit, when Janet and I had gone to the temple, remained. And yet we spoke. I do not know how. But we did. My first question was answered simply, matter of factly, as if he had always been there in attendance on her.

"She came each day to make puja."

His question was unexpected. "Had we been to Varanasi?"

"No. Not yet. But we would be there in six days time."

For three or four minutes he was silent. Then taking something from a recess, he spoke.

"Will you take this rice? Cast it on the waters of the Ganga at dawn. Varanasi was where she was born. I would go there, but I will not get there now, in my lifetime. It is right that she should be remembered."

He gave me the rice. It was small grained, white, and incredibly light, like puffed rice. With commendable practicality the priest tipped his offering from my outstretched palms into a torn corner of old newspaper, twisted it into a cone, and gave me the crude packet.

"This place is filthy and overrun with rats. I thought I was going to die in the bathroom. I was trapped in there with a huge, black rat, which sprang out when I pulled the cistern and neither the rat nor I could get out fast enough. I found the servants at the back and the boy with the pigtail was almost useless, but they changed our room. And, would you believe it, when I made him go into our new bathroom and test the cistern there by pulling the chain, the same thing happened again?" Janet, veteran of infinitely worse experiences, paused for breath, warming to her story telling. "And then I'd seen a fridge at the back, on the veranda. When I went round to find a boy or someone to help, I thought I'd put our bottles of Limca in there to get cold and when I opened the door a whole mess of dirty clothes fell out. This place really is the pits. I can't think how we'll sleep in here. The beds are hard as nails, the sheets are dirty, everything's covered in dust, and what about the rats? Do you have your knife? You'd better sleep with it open."

The place seemed half tolerable after two ounces of Old Natasha (a variant or a rival to the Romanov Extra Smooth we'd found in Agra) had been washed down with warm Limca. We went down to the Shastri Marg and settled on dinner at the Jhansi Hotel. It was one of the worst meals we had yet eaten. Even the Rosy Pelican was flat.

As I placed a flashlight and an open hunting knife on the bedside table, it was hard to believe that my visit to the fort had not been fantasy. Had I been dreaming while I was there? Did it happen? But I had a twist of newspaper with a handful of rice in it in my camera bag, and, forgotten in the excitement of the rats, I still had a red tilak mark on my forehead. It was there when I went to clean my teeth before going to bed.

Six days later, in Varanasi, in the orange light of a pre-dawn sky, Janet and I took a boat out onto the river to discharge my promise to the priest in Jhansi. Our boat was temporarily caught in a cluster of other boats whose occupants were much preoccupied in setting small flowered floats with lights adrift on the Ganges. We persuaded our boatman to pull out into the main stream opposite the Rana Ghat. And there, as the rising fireball cleared the low black line of the eastern bank, I thought of

Lakshmibai, her youth, her fierce loyalty to her princedom and its young heir, and her courage as I scattered my rice on the dark brown flood of the Sacred River. The smoke from the first funeral pyres torched that day hardly rose in the still air as we rowed back to the bank, and the temples, first saffron in the early morning sunlight, slowly turned to gold.

That sunrise was the beginning. I knew then I had to learn more about her than I had done so far, to follow her shadow in those last fateful weeks, and that one day I would write about her.

Arma virumque cano . . .

The lines are Virgil, Publius Vergilius Maro (7–19 BC), taken from the opening line of his epic poem, *The Aeneid.* "I sing of arms and of the hero . . ." The hero was Aeneas, the star of the Trojan war. The wrong sex, maybe, but, like Khayyám, it fits.

Eight

A Place Called Jhansi

So it came about that my Central Indian travels with Jagdishparshad, and my abandonment of Janet and Victoria, was the product of the vow I'd made at dawn on the Sacred River at Varanasi in February 1984. We had no timed plan. I'd told Jag we'd cover three sides of a triangle, east to Kanpur and Lakhnao, southwest to Jhansi, and then northwest to Gwalior and back to Agra. Kanpur and Lakhnao (Cawnpore and Lucknow, to give them their Anglicized names) were on the list because both cities, English garrison towns in 1857, had featured, as had Delhi, as major battlegrounds in the revolt. Janet and I had been to both before, so in a sense it was just touching base for me before Jag and I headed for Jhansi and Gwalior. These gateways to Central India were my real targets, for it was there that I'd pick up the story of Lakshmibai.

Our car was the archetypal Indian car, one of the countless million Hindustan Ambassadors, replicas of the British 1950s Morris Oxford. It was black, outlandishly old-fashioned in appearance, and as comfortable as an unsprung farm cart. Jag, taxi-conditioned, clearly expected me to sit in the back while he drove, but sitting on its hard rear bench would have been purgatory, pretentious, and anti-social. To my surprise everything worked, horn (used constantly), wipers (never used), and lights (used sparingly), and the tires were fine. Oh yes, and we did have brakes, although the accelerator was the standard corrective if we were in danger of collision (which we were frequently). We drove into Kanpur late in the afternoon. It's a major industrial city and the small arms factory and the ordnance factories on the outskirts were emptying, their gates swung wide to release a tidal flood of bicyclists, which placed over a thousand of them on a mile of the Grand Trunk Road. Short of running over people like locusts there was little we could do but progress at pedal pace through the industrial area. With a great deal of horn we shook ourselves free at last. It was a brief period of liberty before we ploughed into the center of a mega-jam with our two remaining bicyclists, who had been pedaling alongside us as if they were limbering up for the Tour de France. It was a brakes rather than accelerator situation, which gives some idea of the gravity of running into a tangle of two trishaws, a taxi, two trucks, and a convoy of ten ox carts. It was dark by the time we were on our way again, but we were the first to extricate ourselves from the chaos. We had an unfair advantage. We had headlights.

Kanpur was set up as a garrison center by the British for it was a nodal point, right on the Grand Trunk Road and on the Ganges, a third of the distance from Delhi to Calcutta. In 1857 Cawnpore, as it was then known, was the scene of one of the many last-ditch stands made by a British garrison when their Indian soldiers turned against them. The murder of women and children taken captive there spurred widespread retaliation, as did the report of a treacherous ambush in which the garrison survivors, having been given a Safe Pass and boats to take them down the Ganges, were killed. The first tragedy was mindless, random violence, directly attributable to two Muslim fanatics. The official report on the second never rang true to my mind, and I wanted to walk the course of events with Jag.

Accepting a truce after a three-week siege, the 450 survivors in the garrison were offered boats to take them down the Ganges to territory still in British hands. The offer was accepted. Escorted by armed mutineers, the refugees, who had been allowed to keep their weapons, filed down a gully that ran into the Ganges at a place called Satichaura Ghat. Some forty boats were waiting for them. They waded out to the boats. A bugle sounded, and the boatmen jumped into the river to get ashore. Sensing treachery, the British opened fire at the enemy soldiers on the bank, who returned fire. Only five British soldiers escaped down river and reached safety. The women and children, about two hundred by most counts, were captured.

I have an 1857 engraving of it. The action depicted is, of course, imaginary, but the setting has hardly changed. There's a little riverside temple dedicated to Shiva on the bank of the river, and the gully down which the garrison survivors made their way from captivity to the promised, waiting boats. There were monkeys playing in and around the trees and the temple buildings as Jag and I, walking the route, arrived at Satichaura Ghat. The Ganges is suddenly there, under your feet, a flat, immense brown flood of water. Almost as if a reenactment had been staged for us, two boats were beached beneath the temple steps, both of them the same heavy, cumbersome river barges they called "budgerows" in 1857.

Jag and I sat for half an hour or so outside the temple, and in time I spoke, through Jag, to one of the priests. We talked of small things, of the winter, for it was cold that day, and of the river, and then, hesitantly on my part, of 1857. I knew the place had another name, the mescar ghat, an Indianization of its British re-titling as the "massacre ghat?" The massacre? What had happened? The priest disappeared and about ten minutes later came out with an old, atlas-sized book. It was not printed, but page after page of handwritten script like a journal, which he started to read. Jag's translation was sporadic, but clear:

> ". . . The boats had been brought to this place. They had boatmen who did not want to go on down the river. The British started to get on board. A horn was sounded to tell the boatmen to leave the boats. The boatmen jumped from the boats. The British shot at them. When the boatmen were shot the soldiers on the bank were angry and opened fire at the British without orders. When he saw the fighting start Nana Saheb told them to save the women and children . . ."

It was much as I had thought. A fatal mistake on both sides. In this case exhausted, paranoid soldiers had opened fire prematurely, fearful that they were being ambushed.

Who was Nana Saheb? The answer leads circuitously to Lakshmibai, Rani of Jhansi. Nana Saheb was the adopted son of the last Mahratta ruler, the Peshwa Bajirao II. Mahratta territory was Madhya Pradesh in Central India and as the British takeover of India continued, Mahratta power, an obstacle to expansion, was broken. Bajirao, forced to surrender his lands in exchange for a stipend, was separated from his people and confined to exile in Bithoor under the watchful muzzles of the British cannon in Kanpur, just twelve miles away. He died in 1851. The succession of his adopted son, Nana, entirely legal by Hindu custom, was ruled invalid, the title revoked, and the pension cancelled. Nana Saheb, at the age of 27, became a private citizen in a gray world of dispossession, neither a Prince of Moghul India, nor a Maharajah of the British Raj, which yet lay in the future.

Manakarnika, the daughter of Bajirao's chief adviser, had been born in Varanasi in 1835, but was brought up amongst the children of his household. At one time it was thought that she was intended as Nana Saheb's bride, but at the age of seven she was married to Gangadhar Rao, the aging Maharajah of Jhansi. The ceremony was a formality. She changed her name, following custom to honor her new status as a Maharani, and took the name of Lakshmibai, after Lakshmi, the goddess of fortune, beauty, success, prosperity, and destiny. Lakshmi's celebration is Divali, the October Festival of Lights, when all houses are whitewashed when the monsoon season ends, and oil lamps are lit everywhere to invite Lakshmi to bless the new year.

Bride she might have been, but her marriage, and her sex, was immaterial in childhood. All the children of Bajirao's court were taught to ride a horse, use a sword, and swim. Mani, it was said, was better than any of them, and could ride like a demon. She was stunningly attractive well before puberty and her looks stayed with her. At the age of sixteen the marriage was consummated. The year was 1851. Lakshmibai had a child, who died three months later. The Rajah, fearing he would have no heir, adopted a five-year-old boy who was named Damodar Rao.

Lakshmibai took the boy to her heart. Two years later the Raja of Jhansi died. The British ruled the succession of Damodar Rao invalid, appropriated the State of Jhansi as it had no heir, and allowed the Rani of Jhansi a pension. She protested. She was ignored, but permitted to continue living in Jhansi.

The ultimate tragedy of Bithoor was that she and Nana Saheb, eleven years her senior, did find partnership, but only in linking to fight the British. Two others from her childhood days joined them: Tantya Tope, her riding and arms instructor, and Nana Saheb's nephew, Rao Saheb. I think it certain that Nana Saheb had no hand in the outbreak of mutiny in Kanpur, and that he brokered the cease-fire and the evacuation plan. He and the others in the

Bithoor group were railroaded by events during 1857 into taking up arms against what they saw as the total conquest and despoilment of their country.

❖   ◆   ❖

On the road from Kanpur to Lakhnao, which Jag and I were taking, it was said that between the two cities there was not a tree that was not black with the bodies of hanging Indians. We didn't talk of this, not then, for somehow it seemed too close to both of us. In 1858, when Lakhnao was recaptured by the British, the scale of retaliation exceeded the punishment Kanpur had suffered. A city of half a million, Lakhnao had been called "more beautiful than Rome, Athens, or Constantinople" by William Howard Russell, the Indian correspondent of the *London Times*. Emily Eden wrote it was "such a place the only residence I have coveted in India. I am sure this was the Garden of Delights." You will find little trace of what they praised today, for the city was totally destroyed within the year.

It was cold in Lakhnao and long before the sun was close to the horizon the light faded as mist and smog gradually completed a total eclipse of the city. A double string of street lights came on along the road paralleling the banks of the Gomti River and other weaker lights showed faintly elsewhere. Snow was falling in the Gharwal Hills of Western Uttar Pradesh, and temperatures dropped to near freezing over the Gangetic Plain. Within half an hour the streets were deserted: no pavement life, no traffic flow, only occasional trishaw drivers who appeared like wraiths out of the mist, the ends of their turbans wrapped round their faces as if the very air was poisonous, and disappeared again. Beneath my window, in a triangular patch of scarred bare earth, two dogs were circling each other on the point of mating, but the premature gloom had unsettled them and they went their separate ways.

❖   ◆   ❖

In 1857, five generations back in my family, Captain Thomas Fourness Wilson of the 13th Bengal Native Infantry had been posted to the staff of Sir Henry Lawrence, the British Administrator for the State of Oudh, in Lucknow, Lakhnao as it is today. The British had already lost Delhi. Twenty-three other garrisons were threatened. At that time the prognosis for British India was not looking so good. Sir Henry, far from dynamic, refused to recognize a state of emergency for fear of precipitating a crisis, but he did open the gates of the

Residency's thirty-seven-acre compound as a refuge for anyone in the British community who felt threatened, and their followers.

Soldiers of Thomas Wilson's regiment, loyal to him, had warned him that the Indian troops had resolved to kill the British. The revolt was planned to start at 9:00 pm on 30 May 1857. The mention of precise time may seem curious in a period when wrist watches were unknown, and indeed none of the Indian population counted time, other than by the sun. But it made sense if your intention was to co-ordinate a garrison-wide uprising, for every evening at nine a gun was fired as a time signal. Sir Henry refused to believe his staff officer, and took no preventive action. That night Captain Wilson, with others, was dining with Sir Henry. The time gun was fired. The table was silent. Listening. There was no abnormal noise. They waited. Nothing. Sir Henry turned to his discredited staff officer:

"Your friends are not punctual."

At that moment there was the crackling of distant musket fire and distant shouting. As they reached the steps of the Residency to see what was going on, the first flames were shooting into the air from the cantonment area.

By the end of June they were under siege in the Residency, a siege that was to last 140 days. They were taking casualties continually from gunfire and musket fire. One of the earliest of these was Sir Henry himself, who against advice had not moved his quarters to safety in the vast basement area of the building.

> **"On the morning of 2 July he [Sir Henry] was resting on his bed, having made his customary rounds of inspection, when another shell exploded in the room, filling the air with smoke, masonry, and brick dust. Captain Wilson [thrown to the floor by the explosion, concussed and wounded] called out 'Sir Henry, are you hurt?' There was no reply. The question was repeated twice; and at length Sir Henry murmured softly 'I am killed.' As the dust gradually cleared Wilson 'saw that the white coverlet of the bed was crimson with blood' . . ."**

I quote from Christopher Hibbert's, *The Great Mutiny India 1857*. Only thirty-two percent of the nearly three thousand who had taken shelter in the Residency compound survived. One of the survivors of the siege described it as "a season in hell." At the end of it all there was not a wall, not one pillar, not one beam, that did not bear the scars of musket balls and shrapnel. The seven hundred men of the only British battalion in the garrison were the backbone of the defense of the Residency.

The lineal descendant of this unit was the 1st Light Infantry, which, at one time, I commanded. Every regiment in the British Army takes great pride in its silver, collections that have been built up, through good fortune or the loot of war, over two hundred years or more. In the siege of Lucknow, as the situation got desperate, everything that came to hand was used to plug the gaping holes in the walls of the Residency. These were days and nights of desperation when the value of any material lay solely in its resistance to shot and shell. An encyclopaedia, it was discovered, could stop a musket ball within 100 pages; regimental silver was additional packing, and used as such. Some of it survived. To this day one great silver soup tureen has been kept by the regiment as it was, somewhat dented after the siege, and patently useless with a musket ball hole straight through it. We were stationed in Hong Kong in 1976 and one evening I was entertaining the Governor and other dignitaries. I sat, as custom dictated, with this prized regimental relic on the dining table in front of me. One of our guests, not at all taken by the crumpled and damaged pot, said:

"Why don't you get it repaired while you're here? There are good silversmiths in Hong Kong, you know."

I woke at six to a total white-out. The dogs were back but the female turned on the male suddenly and drove him off, whimpering. The river was invisible, as was the embankment road, there was no traffic, nothing moving anywhere. Lakhnao, city of a million, was in suspension, in a spell. So much for my plans to take photographs as the first sunlight touched the Residency, and arrive in the Dilkusha, the garden of the Heart's Delight, early enough to find it backlit by low slanting eastern light. I settled to my writing. An hour later I could hear the first automobile horns and the build-up of traffic, and I put away my notebook.

It was time to head for Jhansi. We were jammed for a while in a narrow street. A motor scooter and its two riders were the center of attraction in a swarm of bicyclists, and as we inched forward we saw the scooter rider, a young Indian in jeans, trying to extricate himself from the bicyclists, but getting little help. His passenger, an equally young, nubile, and attractive girl, was sitting sidesaddle behind him, clinging to his waist like a frightened koala. Unlike her boyfriend she was dressed in Indian clothes, a sari skirt and a short, thin, skin-tight silk choli that left her arms and her midrift bare to within six inches of her armpits. Little about her well-formed superstructure was left to the imagination. The surrounding bicyclists, all of them Muslim, were clearly in a spasm of excitement at the random catch that had strayed into their pack. You didn't need a degree in psychology to see how the coexistence of Hindu and Muslim could, so easily, be broken in one incident.

By the time we passed Lakhnao Railway station traffic was heavy. Understatement. How can any nation tolerate such urban bedlam day after day after day? You start with streets that are too narrow and in poor shape, then mix bicyclists, trishaws (both pedal-powered and more upmarket versions with two-stroke engines), and the dreaded tempos (the grotesque and terrifying auto-rickshaw variants, which look like motorized black metal aardvarks). Every vehicle is overloaded: taxis, cars, buses, trucks, bullock carts, ox carts, camel carts, barrows, mopeds, scooters, and motorcycles. Add in the laden camels, wandering cows, bemused homeless buffalo, scavenging pigs, and pi-dogs. Superimpose the tongas, pony traps, and farm carts, together with countless pedestrians, most of whom clearly accept that sudden death under the wheels of a vehicle is unavoidable, if it is in your karma.

Very much part of the scene are the curbside stalls of the food vendors and the families squatting cooking on the roadside with children defecating in the monsoon drains beside them, men urinating against any convenient wall, while others tout for business. Small groups, quite oblivious of everything around them, squat and talk with their neighbors. All around the horns are blaring. Everyone ignores them. Urchins dart through the near-stalled traffic on endless errands and small boys chase stray goats while groups of schoolchildren, the girls in neatly pressed skirts and blouses and the boys always in shorts, swim through the chaos, small darting black-eyed shoals always blue and white, but sometimes gingham. Occasionally the children, either late for school or with affluent parents, are packed fifteen to a gharri, a horse-drawn carriage, or pass by in multiples of seven clinging to tempos or trishaws. There is no discipline in this scene; there is no rule of the road. How could there be? Pairs of police occasionally pass through, in greatcoats and scarves if it's as cold as it was in Kanpur and Lahore, armed with 1914 Lee Enfield rifles or carrying lath-is, long bamboo canes weighted with metal, but they show no interest in their surroundings. What's the annual toll from road deaths in India? I think it works out to around a hundred a day, but I can't remember my source, or vouch for its accuracy.

Jag was talking about racial issues. Clearly the girl on the scooter was on his mind. "A Hindi family has two to three children. A Muslim has ten to eleven. Ask him how he will provide for them all and he will tell you 'God will provide.' But God cannot look after all these people." We were bouncing along behind a truck at that time with a large sign on its tailgate IF MARRIED DIVORCE SPEED. As soon as a gap opened in the traffic both the truck and ourselves, like a dinghy in its wake, were off like greyhounds, none of us in the divorce stakes.

The trucks are driven with suicidal dedication: horn and pure blind courage count for everything. If your half of the road is blocked, you take the other half, even on a divided highway. If you drive in India you must accept that some of your fellow road users may have a mental agility that's less than razor sharp, and many have problems with both the steering and the maneuverability of their vehicles. The eight-year-old boy driving a double bullock cart on the crown of the road. The bicyclist carrying a concrete park bench on his bicycle. This kind of scenario is no one-off. There are endless repetitions, time and time again, the drama heightened by the ceaseless blaring of car and truck horns.

After two hours we stopped at a roadside dhaba for tea. Jag was still talking. ". . . Some Muslim peoples are getting help from Pakistan. Only in those places there is trouble." Which places? The boy rinsed our glasses in a 44 gallon drum of frequently used washing up water, dried them on the hem of his dhoti, which was grey with dirt and its use as a dishcloth, and poured the premixed tea into our glasses. It was hot and thick, sweet with sugar and caramel with buffalo's milk. Jag was still waist deep in places with trouble. I tried to talk of driving in India, but it was dismissed as nothing worth attention: "You need three things. Good luck, good horn, and good brakes." The order of priorities was his: survival was a matter of karma, not of prudent braking. We returned to our discussion of the Indo-Pakistan border and Kashmir as we drove on at breakneck speed, hand on horn, towards Jhansi.

The orange-red sun, a massive fireball, was setting behind the whale-back ridge to the west of Jhansi. In the east the near-full moon was rising, and the silhouettes of the palm trees in the fields looked like inverted Spanish exclamation marks against the pale sky. The city, and the fort beyond it, was partly obscured by smoke rising from cooking fires all over the city. From our Jehu-like progress in heavy traffic on the open road we were reduced to near-paralysis in crowded streets. There the whole world seemed to have business at that hour on the pavements, and on the road itself, quite oblivious of the near-gridlocked vehicles. Eventually we reached the Jhansi Hotel on Shastri Marg.

Jag refused my offer of a room, but we ate together in its gloomy dining room. The food was as bad as it had been when Janet and I had dined there six years before. It even took the edge off the Rosy Pelican beer. The bedroom door locks were impressive, massive brass padlocks, the kind a pirate would put on his treasure chest. My bedroom wall, alongside the single narrow bed, was splattered with the blood of mosquitoes or bed bugs. There was no water. There was "running" only in the morning I was told, but I could have a bucket of water from the kitchen. I'd gone for my bucket in the nick of time, for the power failed just as I'd undone my padlock.

It was cold that night, the kind of night when you put your clothes on rather than take them off, and first light came as a merciful relief. It was also a relief to discover that the forecast "running" was no empty promise. True, it was an eight-foot vertical cascade from a gigantic ceiling shower rose, but it was warm. I could hardly bear to get out on to the cold concrete but screwed up my courage, and turned the shower off. The controls came away from the wall in my hand. Shaving was a tad difficult, for the "running" came out from a pipe into a hand basin which had no plug. I returned to the shower to shave, but that was pointless. Had I forgotten? It was now totally inoperative. Just then we had another power failure. I went to the dining room. Jag joined me within minutes looking fresh, refreshed, and clean.

"Where did you find to sleep?" I asked, with admiration, and some envy.

"Nowhere." he said. "There was nowhere. I slept in the car."

In early 1858, realizing that a British force would soon come to take retribution against Jhansi, Lakshmibai decided to fight. She wins star status from that moment, demonstrating a tactical instinct that can rarely be achieved by book learning, a dynamism that carried everyone with her, and the courage that reinforces even the lame with iron determination. Jhansi was brought to a state of siege preparedness quickly, efficiently, and effectively. Old guns were recommissioned, new guns were forged. Soldiers were trained. Even women volunteered and were trained as troopers and gunners, and in the end fought alongside their men. Supplies were laid in. The immediate countryside around the walls of Jhansi was leveled so that there was nothing to offer shelter or shade to a besieging force. Tantya Tope and Rao Saheb, asked for help, came close to disrupting the British approach to Jhansi but their spoiling move came too late. At the end of March they made a second attempt to relieve Jhansi, but despite superior numbers, they failed. Lakshmibai was on her own.

The siege of Jhansi lasted seventeen days, during which the continual pounding of the British guns caused considerable damage to the city and the outer defenses of the fort, and resulted in about sixty casualties a day among the defenders. The British assault started on April 3 and was directed at the city, not the fort. The attackers had to fight desperately over four days for every yard they gained, and as the street fighting swept in towards the City Palace, Lakshmibai was in the forefront of the counterattacks. By the end of the day the Palace was in British hands. Lakshmibai had withdrawn to the fort, and early in the night was persuaded to escape from Jhansi to live and fight another day. The popular belief is that she tied the boy Rajah to her back with a wide sash and, vaulting the walls of the fort on her horse, made good her escape cutting her way through the besieging pickets. Another version of her escape has it that she fought her way out through the north gate of the city, the Banderi Gate.

However she went, her escape was remarkable. With a small group of companions, and it seems beyond doubt that Damodar Rao was strapped to her back, she fought her way to freedom through the besieging forces. Later, sword still in hand, she cut her way through a cavalry troop who caught up with her at Banda. At midnight on April 5 Lakshmibai reached Kalpi, where she joined Rao Saheb and Tantya Tope. She had ridden 102 miles in 24 hours through rough, rock-strewn, hilly country in 115-degree-Fahrenheit heat; and she had fought hand to hand through desperate opposition for the first twenty miles of her route.

Jag and I had been to the fort and decided the one weak spot Janet and I had identified, where the forty-five-degree hillside rose to within a tall man's height of the parapet, was an unlikely escape route, for the ground was broken with boulders. Could you take it at night? At a full gallop? Surely not. She must have been let out through the Banderi Gate. Perhaps if we went to the Rani Mahal, other fragments of those seventeen days might became clear. The Rani Mahal was her city palace, the residence she had been allowed to retain, where she had made her final stand in the streets. Jag went ahead to turn the car around. As I wandered through the deserted fort on my way back to the main entry the same troop of rhesus monkeys circled out to threaten me, still led by a big old male.

We cast around with some difficulty in the bazaar area and made our way out towards the Lakshmi Gate, and back into the city again. No one we asked had heard of the Rani Mahal. Then I saw a faded yellow facade facing a congested square, northeast of the fort in the old city. Above the stone windows were carved peacocks and fans, her decorative emblems, but the rest was all decay. The building was formed around a central courtyard that was in use as an archaeological dumping ground of stones and statues, but no apparent restoration was in hand. "Palace" was a deceiving title. Town house, or maybe city mansion would have been more accurate. There was nothing of grand design and impressive size there.

"Jag, let's go to her temple now."

"Back to the fort?"

"No. No. The water temple. The one by the tank. The Lakshmi temple. It was her Jhansi temple, wasn't it?" We had no reason to return to her private temple. We'd already been there. The priest, I hoped, would now rest content that I had carried out his wishes in Varanasi.

Once again we passed through the Laxmi Gate and took the narrow road to the lake, to the Lakshmi Bai Talabe. The outer wall of the temple was blank and we passed through a narrow entrance into the temple courtyard. No one was there, and then an old woman came out. What was the name of the temple? I had doubts that we had found the right place. The Maha Lakshmi Temple. Jag intervened to explain more, to talk of the Rani, and to ask: "Was it her temple? Did she come there?" The answer was affirmative. Yes. Each day she was in Jhansi. She came from the Rani Mahal.

I was led up a steep staircase into the temple. In an inner shrine the statue of the goddess Lakshmi was dressed in red like a Catholic Virgin, and around the shrine were tiles with peacocks. The priest was there, and I made puja and left, quietly. Back in the courtyard, as I was retrieving my shoes, the old woman started to talk again. There was a tunnel from the fort to the temple. That was how the Rani had escaped. I knew few, if any, forts or castles were built without a secret exit, normally a tunnel. I checked the distance. It was too great. It would have been a colossal mining undertaking in that terrain. But a shorter exit tunnel? That was entirely probable. That I could believe.

Outside, at the edge of the tank, we found an old boatman, half-blind, with a heavy, awkward boat, which looked as if it had been modeled on an army assault craft and fabricated from ship plate. Slowly he rowed us out so that I could take photographs of the Maha Lakshmi Temple, and of Jhansi, and slowly, hardly making way, we turned and came back to where we had embarked.

"What should I give him?" I asked Jag.

"Be good, Sahib." The title was not a word he often used, or one that I encouraged. "He is an old man and he has nothing." It was a lesson in humility and compassion.

Jhansi was looted, torched, and nearly totally destroyed. No male over the age of sixteen years was spared, and many women and children suffered the same fate. Lakshmibai's father fell into British hands some days later, having escaped from Jhansi in the final phase of the siege. As soon as he was identified he was taken back there and hanged in the Jokhan Bagh.

On 28 April 1857 Lieutenant William Nicholl of the Bengal Artillery wrote from Saugor, just south of Jhansi, to his sister Selina in England:

"I hear that at Jhansi there was indiscriminate slaughter and that some 5000 was about the number of enemy that were killed. I only wish the Rani had been caught and given over to the Europeans to be disposed of in such a way as they would consider best. She would then have only received one hundreth part of what she deserves to suffer, and as for "Nana Dhoudoo Pant" [Nana Saheb] the arch fiend, there is nothing sufficiently horrible in this world to scourge him with for he has certainly surpassed his Satanic master in his diabolical duplicity and cruelty. May God in his infinite mercy deliver the earth of such wretches. The weather is now hot, the thermometer at 90 degrees in this house . . . what it is under canvas (120 degrees or more) for Europeans it is fearful to contemplate."

Nine

The Gwalior Road

 I didn't expect to find any visual evidence of 1858 in Kalpi. The rebel leaders had chosen to fight a battle there that should have gone in their favor, but it turned into a disaster. There would be no traces of the engagement. What I was searching for was just one place. There had been a house there, I knew, on the bank of the Yamuna (Jumna) River where the Indian leaders and Kumar Singh, the Rajah of Patna, had met after the fall of Jhansi to decide their next course of action. I wondered how they'd arranged the meeting. The British, by then, were stringing telegraph lines over India, as well as setting up signal stations and using a system of couriers. The passage of information, for them, was almost immediate, certainly within twenty-four hours anywhere within Northern India. How did Lakshmibai get in touch with Tantya Tope and Rao Saheb? On 4 April 1858 how did they know that she was on her way to Kalpi expecting to meet them there? Could we find their meeting place if we asked around? Jag was doubtful.

"These people are just villagers. They are not knowing anything. They do not even know the next village."

I was sure that somewhere there must be some residual memory, some oral record handed down. If we asked enough people? We started asking and drew blank after blank, and then suddenly struck gold. We had stopped to question a man who was walking towards Kalpi with a basket of vegetables. We'd already been through the village once and were now retracing our route, trying again. "Rani Jhansi?" he repeated. We were on the Kanpur road at that point on the approach to a new road bridge over the river and he pointed to the right, to the distant bank. All we could see were two pylons near a belt of trees. There was no sign of a house or any kind of building. It was there, he assured us. There, over the river.

We crossed the bridge. There was a bluff on the right and half-hidden above it, in the trees, was the dome of a cupola, visible only if you were travelling in that direction, towards the south. We bumped up an approach track. The cupola turned out to be a Chandella dome (the Chandellas a thousand years back had pioneered Indian architecture and not the least of their achievements were the well-known, highly sexual temple carvings at Khajuraho). The simple dome was almost swallowed in the square mass of a larger, later, building with nine-foot walls, set on a series of brick terraces high above the river. If it was the right place, it was an ideal refuge. The site was isolated from the town, impossible to surprise, easily defended, had good escape routes, and clearly offered sufficient accommodation and space to house more than one retinue. It had to be right. I was certain that it was right.

A family who appeared to be caretakers were living in an outhouse to one side of the main building, which was half-shuttered, empty, unused. What had it been before its lapse into dereliction? A Rest House? The caretakers could not say. I went in and took an interior staircase to the roof to look out over Kalpi to get my bearings, and then went down to the first of the terraces to read my notes to see if I'd overlooked some clue that could give me a positive identification. Jag had wandered off, and was poking around on his own. Suddenly he called me.

As I turned around the corner of the outer wall, he pointed to a small dulled plaque that was fastened there, clearly elated with delight at his discovery. The inscription was in Hindi. He translated it slowly. The leaders of India's fight for independence had met there in April 1858. He read the names: Rao Saheb, Tantya Tope, and Lakshmibai, the Rani of Jhansi.

Far below us, on a flat sandspit of island in the gentle curve of the Yamuna, an ant-like file of men was stacking reeds to form windbreaks or embankments around three parallel rectangular fields, still rich with silt from the bounty of the last monsoon. The reflected sky made the river pale blue, the color of a low-grade sapphire, and on each bank the still-green land stretched away into infinity. There was no wind, no noise, just absolute stillness. We rested on the terrace, and for a long time neither Jag nor I spoke. Was it ever peaceful there for Lakshmibai? I put my camera and my notebook away in my backpack.

❖ ◆ ❖

Sir Hugh Rose, who had taken Jhansi, was hard on the rebels' heels. The rebel alliance fought an unnecessary and disastrous battle with British troops some forty miles out from Kalpi on the Jhansi road, and fell back on Kalpi, with the British hard on their heels. It was perfect ground for a defensive battle, with a heartbreaking tangle of ravines to the south and east, and the walls and buildings of some eighty-four temples in the Kalpi area, which could be used to wear down and exhaust an attack. If ever there was a battle that could have been won, the Bithoor team had it made at Kalpi; but Nana Saheb couldn't see it, and Rao Saheb lost his nerve. In desperation Lakshmibai led counterattacks, "fell on them like a tigress," getting to within twenty feet of the British cannon, but it was too late. It would not have been surprising if the rebel alliance had ended at that point, and the leaders had sought personal safety, splintering to find refuge somewhere in the Indian sub-continent. But somehow, probably through the sheer charisma of Lakshmibai, the union endured.

There never was one single India. In the north, south of the Hindu Kush and the Himalayas, there are the mountain tribal areas, Kashmir, and the whole sweep of the Nepalese frontier until you reach Sikkim and Bhutan. The British found no amount of "pacification," be it through bribery or punitive expeditions, could ever knit these peoples into passivity and total subjugation. The northern frontier always remained a place apart, albeit a good training ground for soldiers. The Punjab and the Gangetic Plain is very different territory. Other than the great rivers there are no physical barriers, and the rivers themselves are natural lines of communication. This area is the heartland of the wealth of India.

South of this great central plain, the country changes dramatically. In the north it's high, broken country, difficult to cross, and difficult to tame. In the west the Malabar coast is almost isolated by the mountain range of the Western Ghats, and in the east, the Eastern Ghats similarly parallel the Coromandel coast. The area between these two ranges is a high tableland, set within mountain walls and broken by deep valleys, jungle, and its share of desert. These broken lands became the preserve of the most ancient India, the India of the Ramayana. The subjugation of the central and southlands was too much, even for the great Akbar.

The key to successful insurgency was a fine appreciation of the fault lines in the make-up of India. Lakshmibai knew it intuitively. The set piece battles for the cities were pointless. Hold the key forts. Ensure the whole countryside was with your cause, and use geography and climate to advantage. Operate against your enemies in lightning strikes, and make the attrition such that it was not worth the cost to attempt to subdue Central and South India. Jhansi and Kalpi should never have been lost; but could be recovered. There was one fort, yet uncontested, which was the key to a new start. Which was it? The answer was the Gwalior. It was the only fortress of strategic importance, the Ticonderoga of Central India. There was one additional factor in the Rani's appreciation. It was the end of May. The onset of the monsoon was due in mid-June. When the rains came it would halt all British military activity until October, for they would not be able to move their guns and stores out of their camps. There was no time to be lost. They headed for Gwalior.

❖   ◆   ❖

We too were heading for Gwalior, going the way Lakshmibai could not have gone, taking the road back to Jhansi first. She had taken her team, and her soldiers, cross-country over a land she must have known well. We didn't stop in Jhansi, but made our first stop some sixteen miles later. There, on your right if you're driving from Jhansi to Gwalior, a vast, monolithic palace complex standing high on a ridgeline dominates the distant horizon. It's the deserted palace of Bersingh Dao, the seat of the rajas of Datia. We stopped. As I knelt and focused my camera, a girl child in a tattered cotton shift came out of the camel thorn at the roadside and stared deep into my lens, grave and motionless. Our eyes were linked, bonded by sixteen elements of convex and concave glass and three reflecting mirrors, and I felt as if my very soul was being examined. Then she broke the contact, and ran off. We left the car by the roadside and walked into a pocket city. Datia could be taken as quintessential rural India, the India you expect but which most tourists would rather not experience at close hand, except through the windows of a tour bus. It had everything: an outlying ring of satellite villages with their fields and wells, the remains of city walls, temples, that vast, abandoned palace, and a way of life that could hardly have changed significantly in a millennium. The noise of the trucks passing on the Gwalior–Jhansi road was muted and irrelevant. Or were they irrelevant?

Slowly changes are coming. Those trucks bring paraffin stoves, and audio contact with an outside world, cheap radios, and batteries. The one-time isolation and self-sufficiency of the India village is now a mirage. If your family can afford a paraffin cooking stove, no longer will you, the woman of the house, and your daughters, have to spend hours combing the fields for cow dung and forming it into peat-like fuel patties. Your husband will not have to scour the countryside cutting branches from every tree for firewood. The cow dung can remain in the fields as fertilizer, and the trees can grow. In time the trees will hold fertile soil in the monsoon season better than any bund, they give shade, and extended tree cover may, in time, slowly change the climate. Are there any drawbacks? Yes, the cost of buying your stove and the realization that it doesn't stop there, for you are joining another world, linking in to an economy dependent on cash flow to sustain it. You have to pay for your fuel. And there are less obvious dangers in adapting to new ways:

"Rekha (22), wife of Ram Kumar, a resident of Amousi village under Sarojini Nagar police station, was killed when her clothes caught fire from the stove here this morning."

The brief report was in the *Times of India*. It is not an unusual occurrence.

We walked back to the road to continue on our way to Gwalior. In a perverse sense I was not displeased to see Datia's palace, all seven floors of it, in dereliction, for Datia had ignored Lakshmibai's call, from Jhansi, for help. Perhaps it was a just comeuppance, or you could say that it was the Ozymandias factor at work.

It's about sixty miles from Jhansi to Gwalior, and apart from two places, Datia, and Sonagir, there's little on the route that might prompt you to stop. You're back to the perils of the open road, with that thundering overladen truck GIVE ME HORN OK? holding the crown of the narrow tarred surface ahead of you. There's no way you can overtake, even with the invited horn, for the road makers had saved money on the hard top; it's close to single lane, and the verges are sand. It was a relief when, at roughly the half-way point, we reached Sonagir. There, travelling the way we were going, a great ridge crowned with white temples came up on the left. Against the brown rock and burnt sienna of the landscape and the cloudless blue wash of the sky the temples looked surrealist if not Dadaist, with prayer flags fluttering in the heat wind. Apart from the temples on the skyline no one, and nothing else, seemed to be there. We turned towards the ridge, crossing the railway line that parallels the road at Sonagir, and pulled into a parking area under the shoulder of the whale-back, where we found the entry gate to the temple area. There was a man on a bench by the gate reading a newspaper. No one else was in sight, and no other vehicles. Our lone fellow human being had horn-rimmed glasses, and the dignity, as well as the face and look, of a Boston banker. He was stark naked. I greeted him with deference, a greeting he too, equally formally, returned. As he returned to his newspaper, I took off my shoes to climb the steep concrete path to the temples.

The Jain temples of Sonagir may not be worth the thirty-seven mile journey from Gwalior if you get that far and are going no further, but if you are travelling on to Orchha or Khajuraho you should stop there. I was told that at Holi, the festival of Spring, the place comes alive; but I think I would prefer Sonagir as I saw it then, in the mode of Ernst or Dali, with no one there but the naked newspaper reader with his horn rims, and a backdrop of infinity.

Ten

A Cheval Glass and an Empty Swing

Gwalior was a signal prize if you could win the fort without a shot being fired. The fortress itself crowns a precipitous isolated rock standing quite free of its surrounding plain and the city. The great plug of sheer rock on which the fort is built measures about a mile and a half in length, is comparatively narrow, some 400 yards in width, and rises about 350 feet in height. Decorated with almost frivolous cupolas capping its six guardian towers, the walls of Gwalior are none the less serious defensive works: tall, solid, continuous, and well-built, a vertical extension of the rock face. There's only one entrance to the fortress complex, a steep ascent rising itself within walls, guarded by no less than seven gates, each covered by the field of fire of bastions in the main fortress walls high above. Within the fort there are great underground rooms carved into solid rock offering bomb-proof shelter and three vast tanks holding thousands of gallons of water. Given men, munitions, food, and the determination to hold it, Gwalior was impregnable; and remained so until the advent of air power and weapons of mass destruction. It is the most dramatic and impressive fort in India.

The rock plug of the fortress is circled by relatively level ground on which both the old city and the overspill new city, with its surrounding gardens, were built. To the east and south the Gwalior plain extends for roughly two miles. Then the hinterland is broken by bare low hills, nullahs, and old watercourses. The road from Jhansi runs in from the south through this broken terrain, gaining the plain through a low pass in the hills, a route shared by an irrigation canal. Just to the south of this defile there's a small village, Kotah-ki-Serai. A ravine runs roughly east–west across the road just to the north of Kotah-ki-Serai, but once you are through the circling hills there is nothing to stop you, no obstacles between you and the city. A Hindu temple, a mosque, and the Phool Bagh, a walled garden, all on the outskirts of Gwalior, are just a mile and a half away. In those days these outliers were all in open countryside, the bare desert plain. Today Gwalior's urban crawl has enveloped them, and not one identifiable feature can be picked out from a distance.

❖ ◆ ❖

The British soon heard that Tantya Tope, Rao Saheb, and the Rani of Jhansi were on their way to Gwalior. No one was under any illusion that this was just another dash for the refuge of another fort. The Maharaja of Scindhia, the ruler of Gwalior, had stayed on the British side in 1857 but his loyalty was no more than a pragmatic accommodation to the greater strength of foreign arms. His subjects were less accommodating. His private army had declared their views early and had joined the rebels. Lord Canning, who had taken over as British India's Governor General, made the import of the Rani's move very clear: "If Scindhia joins the Mutiny, I shall have to pack off tomorrow." Scindhia was already on his way to Agra, leaving the gates of Gwalior open. He had paused only to change his clothes, and, hell-bent on haste in his self-preservation, left his mother and his women behind.

There could not have been a more auspicious restart for the Indian rebel leaders. On 3 June 1858 Rao Saheb held a great durbar to proclaim his assumption of power as the ruler of a new Mahratta confederacy. It was a grand public relations show staged for an audience of hundreds with the intention of winning the allegiance of thousands. The ceremonies ran on for two weeks, and it seemed they held all the cards: they had the best fort in India, guns, munitions, fresh troops, and Scindhia's jewels and his treasury were at their disposal.

The durbar and the festivities were a very necessary psychological boost for a revolt that had come within a degree of foundering at Kalpi, but the peacock feathers and the panoply of power must have gone to Rao Saheb's head. Taken up by the delusion of his inaugural sleigh ride, the outside world was forgotten. Lakshmibai was the only one who had the mental agility and the ability to transfer herself into the mind of Sir Hugh Rose. He would, she guessed, lose no time; he would be in sight of Gwalior within days, ready to fight from the first moment of contact. She was right, They had delayed too long.

On the morning of June 17, a British force coming up from Jhansi was five miles to the southeast of Gwalior. Sir Hugh Rose, it was patently clear, was about to play the same game he had played at Jhansi: to take the city first, for it was the soft target, and ignore the fort. If he won the city, the probability was that the fort would be surrendered. Lakshmibai had no options. The most vital factor in defense, choice of ground, had been given away before the first round had been fired. To fight street by street, as they had in Jhansi, would invite the total destruction of the city and the sacrifice of its population. The critical battle would have to be fought east of Gwalior, where she was already extended over a six-mile front with barely two miles of depth to her position. Her situation could not have been worse. It was a nightmare.

The fortress rock, and the fort itself form a magnificent backdrop, and must have done so then, but were useless in the battle that had to be fought. Kotah-ki-Serai and the low hills were outside the range of the fort's guns. I'd photocopied all the 1858 maps of Gwalior I could find, and taking the best of them, I brought the contours to life, coloring in the high ground and marking the roads, the watercourses, and the canal. It was hard to conceive of a worse place to fight a defensive battle.

If I'd been in charge of the Indian side I would have put my toughest and most obstinate commander in the fort with just enough troops to hold it, and told him to lock the doors. I would have abandoned the city, and told its inhabitants to take shelter in the fort before the gates closed, or disappear into the countryside. Then I would have withdrawn out of contact, south, into broken, roadless country. For the next week or so, until the monsoon came, I would have cut the British lines of communication so that the forces in the Gwalior area were isolated. Then, when the rains came and there was no way in which they could move their guns, I would start attacking each position in turn. If the resistance was too great, I'd break off the engagement, disappear into the hills, and then come back and repeat the process, time and time again. Lakshmibai had no chance to think of alternatives. On the morning of June 17 the British were already deep in the broken country, over the Morar River, and had reached Kotah-ki-Serai.

Jag and I left our car parked there by the side of the road. We walked through the village and around the area, finding the features on my highlighted maps. We returned to sit on a low wall on the northern side, facing the ravine. It was the line the British leading elements had reached that day. Gwalior was out of sight, about a mile to our front. We had decided that Lakshmibai had drawn the worst hand you get out of the pack. It was a loser. The only answer was to cut and run. Her solution was sudden, violent, and unconventional. She shelled the British in Kotah-ki-Serai and then charged out from behind the low hills that shielded Gwalior. She caught them by surprise and forced them back, inflicting heavy casualties; but her initiative was never exploited by Rao Saheb and Tantya Tope. There was no move to reinforce her. By nightfall, even though Kotah-ki-Serai was no longer in British hands, the situation was desperate.

The Rani had taken the garden area, Phool Bagh as her center, and the stop line, the point at which an attacking force must be halted. It was fine in theory, but she knew her troops had neither the training nor the discipline to fight a mobile defensive battle. To allow yourself to be beaten back to gain your victory requires brilliant timing, and nerves of steel. The stop line had to be the hills. She counterattacked again on the morning of the 18th, but once again could not sustain the momentum. As the day went on, British gunfire and the hammering of successive attacks started to tell as they forced their way through the Kotah-ki-Serai defile. By late afternoon Gwalior was in front of the attackers with the Rani's forces in plain view. British cavalry were unleashed to charge them, and Lakshmibai met them head-on. Unknown to her enemy, and indeed to most of her own side, she was mortally wounded and carried off dying. The day of June 18th ended with the Phool Bagh still in Indian hands. Lakshmibai died that night.

❖ ◆ ❖

I know of thirteen different accounts of Lakshmibai's death. The stories run from her death under gunfire to suicide. The suicide version is a psychologically complex myth confusing her cremation (which did take place) with an act of self-immolation in expiation of her "treachery," and suggests that having been gravely wounded, she ordered that she be placed on a haystack which was then, at her express command, set on fire. There is an element of embarrassment in many of the British accounts, as if the killing of a young woman in action was unintentional, regardless of her blackened reputation. Much is made of the confusion of close combat, the disguise of her man's clothing, her short hair, and her riding in a man's manner, astride her horse; and the fall-back line was that whoever shot her, or cut her down, probably had no idea who she was. The evasion holds no validity. Lakshmibai had held her front line for two days fighting a spirited, aggressive, and successful defensive battle, due entirely to her personal leadership. Wherever the situation was critical she was there within minutes, leading every counterattack, surrounded by her personal bodyguard and with two female attendants who were with her constantly, riding, like her, armed and astride their horses. The three of them dressed as men not as disguise, but because you could not ride, and fight, wrapped in the clothes of a woman. They were instantly recognizable, wherever they went, more so as Lakshmibai "fought like a tigress," as she had been described at Kalpi.

It was at dusk on the second day of the battle for Gwalior when she met the British breakout head-on. In the hand-to-hand battle she was shot, most probably in the back. Slumped in her saddle she was taken at once from the thick of it. Her close escort dismounted under a tree, and their intention was to carry the Rani to the safety of the fort. One of her female attendants was also mortally wounded in the same action and died there, tearing off her clothes in agony. The British soldiers who found her body said she was "most beautiful." The observation seems voyeuristic, and gross.

The route back to the fort for the small party carrying the Rani was hardly easy going, for there was a wall to their front that surrounded the Hindu temple, and a small nullah had to be crossed before they reached the Phool Bagh. Gwalior, and the safety of the fort, was still far distant. Her rescuers never made it past the Hindu Temple, or maybe they just reached the Phool Bagh. Lakshmibai was lifted over the wall, but she was fading fast, so they decided to go no further. Dying, she ordered that the necklace she was wearing, prize pearls taken from Scindhia's treasury, together with her bracelets and other jewelry, be given to her soldiers, and there is a suggestion that Damodar, her adopted son, was brought to her at that point. It could well have been so. The fighting had ended at nightfall with both sides exhausted. There was a lull. The front line, at least for the night to come, was stabilized. Lakshmibai died. They decided to cremate her at once for there could be no delay: they would be locked in battle again the next morning. Her pyre was built at the edge of a watercourse and fired that night.

Gwalior was not to fall for another three days, but surrender was inevitable; as the news of the Rani's death spread, it was as if the only bright flame of resistance on the rebel side had been extinguished. It had been. It was the end of the Indian Revolt.

Jag and I drove on into Gwalior and parked in what I reckoned was the Phool Bagh area. My 1858 maps were almost useless. Indeed trying to find your way through traffic-choked streets using a map that bore absolutely no resemblance to your surroundings was not only frustrating, but at times near-suicidal. I was finding my way by instinct. Jag and I were giving a fair imitation of kangaroos as we dodged the traffic, I lost my sense of direction, and we had to backtrack for a while; and then we found the Hindu temple. They had intended to take her from there to the fort. Which way would they have gone? Where was the nullah? We found it: a garbage-choked drain that passed under the Jhansi Road in a culvert.

"Jag, it's here. It must be somewhere here that she died and was cremated." And so it was.

Ahead of us there was an iron fence around an enclosure of worn grass, about the size of a small playground. Inside it was a black bronze statue of a woman on horseback in full gallop, sword raised high, on a red ochre pedestal. The central feature of the garden was what appeared to be a white painted tomb on a platform with steps leading up to it. Flowers in tubs flanked the tomb, and a flagpole, with an Indian flag at the mast-head, was at one side. A sign by the gate, at least for us, was superfluous.

A plaque on the memorial tomb paid tribute to her.

CHHATRI OF MAHARANI LAKSHMI BAI OF JHANSI
THIS MONUMENT MARKS THE SITE OF THE
CREMATION OF THE ILLUSTRIOUS AND HEROIC
MAHARANI LAKSHMI BAI OF JHANSI WHO FELL
IN THE BHARAT OF THE FREEDOM WAR OF 1857-58
BORN AT BENARES ON NOVEMBER 19 1835 A D
DIED AT GWALIOR ON JUNE 18 1858 A D
THE MONUMENT WAS CONSTRUCTED BY THE
GWALIOR ARCHAEOLOGICAL DEPARTMENT IN 1929 A D
DURING THE REIGN OF HIS HIGHNESS
JIWAJI RAO SCINDIA ALIJAH BAHADUR OF GWALIOR

Had we gone directly into the center of Gwalior and asked, I am sure we would have found the little park directly. In retrospect, I think it was better to go the way we went, first to walk the course at Kotah-ki-Serai, and then to walk the ground at Phool Bagh, 1858 map in hand. We retraced our path back to our car, and drove through the city to climb the steep approach road, through the entry gates, into the fortress.

Inside the fort the British barrack blocks have fallen into ruin and little else remains of British occupation save for the gun batteries, each one numbered, the guns there still pointing out over Gwalior, and the ammunition stores, also marked and numbered, now long derelict. The fort itself remains a triumph of the combination of splendid defensive architecture and the palace of your dreams, and its temples, the Sasbahu pair, and the Teli-ka-mandir, are early, ninth century, and superb. After our tour Jag and I went back to sitting on the walls overlooking Gwalior, and Jag asked me when we would be starting for Agra. Of course. He would want to return to his family. We had reached the end of our quest, though I needed time to pull my thoughts together.

"What is it? About seventy miles? Something like that? We'll start soon. We'll be there tonight." I reassured him. I knew that I too didn't want to stay in Gwalior. Somewhere close by, perhaps, but not there. Not then. Jag, happy, went off to make the car ready.

High on the walls of the fort you can look eastwards over the urban sprawl of Gwalior and beyond the hills of Kotah-ki-Serai to the endless apparent wasteland of Central India. The heat haze and the dust limits your vision but you can sense the curvature of the earth and you know that out there, far beyond your sight range, the next great plug of rock is Jhansi. Down below you, in the garden that once was called the Phool Bagh, the bankside where the Rani of Jhansi had been cremated was found soon after the battle, but nothing was made of it, most probably for fear that it might become a martyr's shrine. Her tent was also found when the battlefield was cleared. It had in it books, a cheval glass, and an empty swing.

I was ready to leave. I had gone as far as I could go following her path. The tryst I had made six years before in the orange light of dawn at Varanasi was honored.

What happened after June 1858? A sudden capitulation after Lakshmibai's death? Yes and no. Tantya Tope took to the hills as a guerrilla and plagued the British for another year, but was eventually betrayed. He was hanged. Rao Saheb renounced the world and became a mendicant priest, but he too was betrayed in 1862, and taken to Bithoor to be hanged in front of the palace, despite clear evidence that he had played no part in the Kanpur massacres. The nine-year-old boy Rajah of Jhansi, Damodar Rao, was held as culpable for the revolt in Jhansi as his adoptive mother. As punishment he was denied the inheritance due on his coming of age, and the Government of the newly declared British India pocketed the money held in trust for the heir of Jhansi.

Sir Hugh Rose recorded his dismissive judgement of the most remarkable woman in India, who at her death was just twenty-three years old. It ran "The bravest and the best military leader of the rebels. Treacherous, savage, cruel, and licentious, though this lady proved herself, yet one cannot refuse our meed of admiration to her bravery and military qualities."

It wasn't all defamation, but the letters and diaries that take another line are rare. Cornet Combe of the 3rd Bombay Light Cavalry, one of the patrol who intercepted her after her escape from Jhansi, wrote, "She is a wonderful woman. Very brave and determined. It is fortunate for us that the men are not all like her." His letter continued "The poor thing took no part whatsoever in the massacre of the European residents of Jhansi in June 1857. On the contrary, she supplied them with food for two days . . ."

In contemporary comment Lakshmibai's youth and beauty, and the silks, furnishings, and luxury of her own apartments, were used to damn her in British eyes. One diarist, who had met her in early 1857, described her wearing "a dress of plain white muslin, so fine in texture and drawn about her in such a way that the outline of her figure was plainly discernible." Then, with unusual candor for the time in which he wrote, he added, "And a remarkably fine figure she had." British propaganda had it that she was wildly lascivious, a word that was used at the time, meaning depraved, corrupt, and not to be trusted. The vituperative condemnation was infinitely more indicative of the prurience and sexual repression of the Victorian male in India in the second half of the nineteenth century.

After the dust had settled, no one could doubt that the old India would ever return. Temples and palaces were torn down to make way for telegraph lines, railways, canals, and new roads. An Imperial stamp was placed on India, Direct Rule was imposed, and Queen Victoria was declared to be Empress of India. Finally, as a prudent precaution, the size of the British Army in India was doubled, and soldiers went to the compulsory Sunday garrison church services with their rifles loaded. But there were other lessons that had been learned. Missionary activity was no longer actively encouraged; and the surviving princely states, still one third of India, were left as they were. Expansion had gone far enough. An overlordship was certainly established over these states, but the line marking British penetration into India was forever frozen on the line of 1857. But for those who could see it, even then, the writing was on the wall. British power could not last in India.

❖ ◆ ❖

Today, in the book shops of Delhi, Agra, Kanpur, and other cities, you will find stories about the Rani of Jhansi on the children's shelves, for she has been hailed as India's Joan of Arc. In a sense she was, but she was never a national hero, despite a rebranding of the Indian mutiny as the Indian War for Independence.

Why? You are looking at a nation with a history dating back to 2500 BC. A nation divided by geography, ethnic differences, and history into nineteen potentially separatist provinces, and further divided by six main religions, sixteen major languages, 1,400 dialects, fettered in part by the residual bonds of a stratified caste system of almost incomprehensible complexity. We are talking of a nation facing almost insoluble social problems, not the least of which is a birth rate that will take India's population to a thousand million within the immediate future. The fate of a minor tribal princess, who lost her life in a now nearly forgotten insurrection close to 150 years ago, draws no banners. It does not diminish her achievements, and her courage. It is sad, but true.

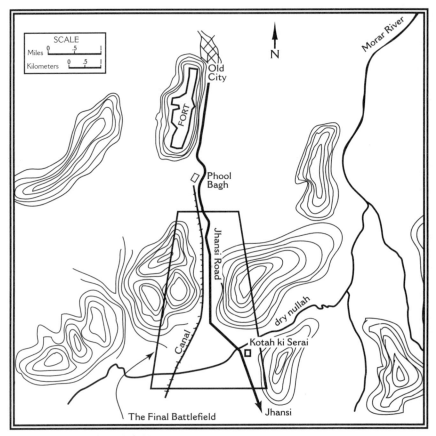

Gwalior. The Final Battlefield

Eleven

A Beach in Goa

In 1510 the Portuguese, the first Europeans to break out of the Atlantic into the Indian Ocean, were fortifying a trading post in Goa. They were to stay there for 451 years. It was not until 1583 that the first English adventurers were scouting India, prudently equipped with letters of introduction to both the Emperor Akbar and the King of China. The Portuguese were not greatly taken by this enterprise and jailed them all when they reached Goa. The English captives were eventually freed on bail, escaped from Goa, and made their way across India reporting with wonder and amazement on temples filled with idols "some be like a cow, some like a monkey, some like peacocks, and some like the devil," war elephants, diamond mines, the abundance of gold and silver, "the great piping and playing" that accompanied the shocking union in marriage of boys of eight or ten to girls of five or six, the force of the monsoon deluge, beggars, holy men, mountains so tall they could be seen at a distance of six days travel, and the lowlands of Orissa in the east where they found "grass longer than a man, and very many tigers."

They saw Fatehpur Sikri at the height of its short occupation as a new Moghul capital and one of their number, William Leader, elected to stay on in Agra in Akbar's service and was at once awarded a house, a horse, five slaves, and a regular pension. It was more than enough to put India on the English map as the equivalent of the Spanish Eldorado, and it was the ecstatic reports of these English adventurers that sowed the seeds of the downfall of Moghul India.

Perhaps the underlying reason for Goa's largely pacific existence was that the Portuguese were content with what they had, and other than a few marginal enlargements and adjustments, stayed out of the takeover stakes for the sub-continent as a whole. Indeed, they even traded their alternative port of Bombay to the British in 1661 as part of the dowry of the Infanta Catherine of Braganza on her marriage to Charles II, and were happy to do it. The Mathrattas rattled the bars of the Portuguese golden cage briefly at the end of the eighteenth century, but they were a pain in the neck to everyone but themselves at that time. As for the British, other than for a moment of angst during the Napoleonic Wars, they stayed clear. By then Goa was a sideshow in any event, for the British controlled the oceans and seas of the world and had a stranglehold on Indian trade. Goa became a sleepy hollow. It was to take the jumbo jet and the western fixation with beach living and suntans before Goa was a name that many people could locate on an outline map of India.

The Portuguese colonization of Goa was in many ways enormously successful. Undoubtedly there was mutual contentment if not mutal profit in the arrangement, which was only twice seriously disputed. Then in 1961 the Indian Government, no longer tolerant of foreign incursion, pulled the WELCOME mat from under their feet.

After Gwalior I needed to pull myself back to the India of the day, and time to go through my notes and add to them before my memory went blank. I needed a change, too, after the barren red ridges and rocky hills of Central India, and had chosen Goa deliberately as a complete contrast.

The change was absolute. As my flight from Delhi landed at Dabolim, Goa's airport outside Panaji, I felt I'd left India. It might have been Malaysia, it could have been the Kenya Coast, or somewhere on the Central American coast. It was the coconut palms, the thatch of the poorer houses, the "Mediterranean" tile roofs of the better houses, the wayside Calvaries and the votive crosses at the crossroads. It was the change in human approach, people suddenly more open, more ready to stop and talk, and the children more friendly, no longer darting shoals of elusive blue and white fish. It was the cleanliness, at first sight a long stride ahead of the rest of India (though later I came to reverse that award, but I think unfairly, for I was on the worst stretch of the tourist coast by then). Above all it was the colors. I'd been living in a world washed of vibrant color, the very land that had led to the identification of khaki as the camouflage for a soldier. In Goa everything is overturned in a riot of viridian green changing to neon green in the paddy fields, the burnt sienna and umber of the raw earth, the blaze of bougainvillea, the red of the laterite dirt roads, and the brilliant white of the churches. It was blinding under full sun. You needed your dark glasses.

I had no clear plan where I was going to stay, only that I wanted to see Old Goa, and then take time off, ideally in a beach-front bungalow if I could find one, to index and organize my notes. So having landed, Panaji, on the doorstep of Old Goa, was my first target. Later, through some inexplicable factor of subliminal orientation, I found myself heading southwards in my exploration and ignored the far north. In retrospect perhaps I should have stayed in the Fort Aguada Beach Resort, right up in the north of Goa, and turned to my maps and notebooks in peace and luxury. I'd become so conditioned to be content with any accommodation a notch or two above rock bottom, that Fort Aguada, stratospherically high in the grande luxe bracket compared to the Jhansi Hotel, had been out of sight. But would I have seen Goa if I'd stayed there?

If you're wise you don't hang around in Panaji, which became the Portuguese capital in the mid-nineteenth century when they moved downriver from Old Goa, which is six miles up the Mandovi estuary. It was difficult to see the advantage of the move, but I'd guess it offered easier access for their ships. Even then they must have had reservations about their new site for a capital, for Panaji, architecturally, is totally without distinction. None the less, I spent two days there, for there's nowhere to stay in Old Goa. Beware of river estuaries. Goa has two great rivers, the Mandovi and the Zuari, which carry the silt and detritus of the interior far out into the sea. They meet at Panaji and if you ever thought of swimming there, forget it.

The first morning, walking back from a visit to the Mahalakshmi temple on the outskirts I stopped at the central maidan to watch a troop of schoolgirls being drilled as if they were army recruits, a sight I hadn't seen in India before. Around sixteen or seventeen years in age, they were dressed uniformly in just-below-the-knee length grey pleated skirts and white blouses, and they all had identical mare's tails of long black hair. Arms swinging shoulder high, they marched and turned, and turned about, the mare's tails swinging out in a flash of black punctuation marks at the turns. Granted it was the only show in town at that moment, but there was something hypnotic about the silent disciplined rhythm and grim concentration of the all-girl squad. Everyone passing the maidan that day stopped to watch. The drill was near faultless, save for one girl in flip-flops who found her footwear ill-suited to the stresses of uneven ground and abrupt 180-degree turns. The others, more prudently outfitted by their wiser or more affluent parents, were wearing sneakers and ankle socks. Before the display was over the crowd splintered suddenly, its collective attention caught by something behind us. There, on the other side of the street, two policeman had cornered a man in the doorway of a shop and were beating him with their lathis as if determined to thrash him to death. After taking unbelievably vicious punishment as he cowered on the doorstep, he escaped by bolting straight through the ring of spectators. Everyone around me appeared well content with both morning diversions, and went their separate ways. I walked on to catch my bus to Old Goa.

It's hard to believe that Goa, the city, was once said to come close to rivaling Lisbon. The one-time city area is fragmented by the main road from Panaji to Ponda, but there's nothing there now. A cathedral. Three other massive churches. An archway. Some scattered ruins. A few walls disappearing into the coconut plantations. There's no trace of landings, docks, streets, or houses. It's extraordinary. It seems the Portuguese were never strong on city planning on a grand scale, domestic architecture, or building their colonial settlements to last forever. All their constructive energy, and the stone work, went into forts and cathedrals. For the rest they must have been content to live in less substantial buildings, to use composite laterite walls and thatched roofs, which would make a cool and watertight house. It's true that this kind of construction wouldn't last two seasons unless the structure was maintained, but the maintenance was simple, easy, and cheap. I thought of Mombasa, Malacca, and Macao. I'd been to all three places. The Portuguese legacy in all of them is much the same. Forts and cathedrals. Not grand squares, avenues, streets, and houses.

I found Old Goa, World Heritage Site though it is, depressing. On reflection I'm not surprised that the Portuguese moved to Panaji, for in Old Goa the banks of the Mandovi River are low lying and claustrophobic. Panaji, if nothing else, offers a suggestion of sea horizon out over Aguada Bay. What does a World Heritage Site imply? Is it no more than a mark of importance, a rating like Michelin's stars awarded as an encouragement to visit the site before it is too late, while the fabric still endures? Or is it the guarantee of a binding commitment on the part of the owner nation for its upkeep and judicious restoration? Unless some funding is made available soon, all one can predict for Portuguese Goa is the almost certain irremediable decay of the churches and the ruination of their frescoes and paintings. The sad museum filled with pictures of the former governors of Goa is a brave attempt, but a monument to every mistake you can make in the museum business. The prognostication for Old Goa is not encouraging. Denigration apart, I got some superb, haunting photographs inside the cathedral, in which the light at that time bleached every color in the spectrum to shades of white gold.

Renting a motorcycle, I set out in search of a better place to stay for the rest of my time in Goa. The search was simplified. Keep to the coast. The interior of Goa is fine, rural, unspoilt, and what most people imagine a tropical countryside to be, but it's not tourist territory and wayside accommodation doesn't appear to be in demand. The change comes along every road or track leading westwards to the coastline from the north-south road, National Highway 17. The beaches of Goa are like the Atlantic beaches of Florida, apparently endless miles of broad sand shelving into shallow water, a continuance broken only by rivers, in this case the rivers flowing down from the highlands of Karnataka. If you were prepared to swim the estuaries, it seems that you could walk forever on the flat, golden sand. It's that sand, the lure of the Arabian Sea, and the fringing palms that attracted tourism, and with it the places to stay.

Have you been to Colva? Drive west from Margoa and you find yourself in a nightmare corridor of jerry-built lodging houses, cheap hotels, houses with rooms to let, bungalows for rent, shops, and stalls selling shalwars, second-hand paperbacks, postcards, tawdry souvenirs, T-shirts claiming IT'S BETTER IN GOA, Tibetan carvings, and provisions. Rarely is any new building finished, and those that are completed are already deteriorating. The Colva road ends at the beach in a great turning circle filled with taxis and their highly vocal drivers, touts, barrow vendors, groups of slicked-up Indian male gigolos waiting to fall in beside any unescorted white girl, and the normal run of human beach sharks. You reach the sand by crossing over the main drainage ditch, a vast evil-smelling monsoon drain filled with garbage in which pigs and pi-dogs are ferreting and fighting. You pass through the zone of the beach bars and restaurants, thick with the stench of deep-frying, get your bearings and try to find out where you are. The vestiges of what was once a fishing village are still there. Some native houses to your right, spread out under the palms. Fishing nets drying, and fish drying (yellow tail and prawns) spread out on jute sacks on the sand. Outrigger-fishing boats are drawn up on the beach, and moored in line, just offshore, is a row of motor fishing vessels. But Colva could be tolerable, it could just be tolerable, but for your own kind. I'd had a long day and had failed to find my magic place. I stayed there.

There's a kind of uniformity to the people you meet on the beach, and a uniform vacuity that suggests, having reached paradise, something has been found missing; doubtless however someone will find a fix and the news will get round. It's a pity that the representatives of the western nations should appear as they do, but there it is, apparently de rigueur. A tie-dyed loose T-shirt or a shalwar, with Rajasthani or Tibétan jewelry, if you are a girl, and a Baluchi or Rajasthani mirrorwork sack bag. Forget shaving if you are a boy, wear your hair shorn or in a pigtail, and earrings. One middle-aged hippie with his thinning hair drawn in a pigtail was sitting on the beach with his girl friend beside him, way less than half his age, naked but for her thong, with immature budding breasts and the hips of a child. She sat like a child at play at the water's edge desultorily moving the sand into little hillocks and then levelling the mounds, time and time again. For over an hour she appeared totally absorbed in what she was doing while he, a little apart, stared at the sea horizon. Neither of them spoke. Then still without a word he rose and walked off, and she, after a flash of irritation at being taken from her game, followed.

Yes, the hippies are still there, camping out and sharing cheap lodgings, but by far the largest foreign continent are the package groups on one-week or two-week holidays. I found a handout in my hotel.

NIGHTLIFE
Evening entertainment is focused almost entirely on some of the larger hotels. You will enjoy traditional Goan and Portuguese folk singing and dancing, and this makes a very colorful and lively spectacle. You can, of course, as an alternative walk to a local beach bar restaurant, known locally as a "shack" where the eating and conversation extend well into the early hours of the morning.

By nine in the evening Colva Beach was dead. Barrows with unsold puri were being wheeled away, the racks of clothing and the jewelery trays were vanishing, and a British tour group was shouting defiance at the world from the compound of a beach bar, knee deep in Kingfisher beer bottles. Back at the Silver Sands Hotel the local Lions Club meeting in the dining room was proving that no nation held a monopoly in partying and the noise level was hitting near-riot strengths; and then the power failed. Absolutely. The effect was magic. For the first time you could see the stars.

I went on searching for my ideal refuge. Benaulim was no good. A concrete and tarmac parking area surrounded by rental cottages. A sign on the beach stated NUDISM IS PROHIBITED but there was little evidence that it was taken seriously. At Fatrade they were building a new Ramada. I went as far south as it seemed sensible to go, at least until I left the tourist strip somewhere north of Cabo de Rama, and then retraced my route, having failed to find anywhere I fancied.

By midday it was hot, and I took a dirt road down to the beach near Karmane. A drinks shack was set up about three hundred yards back from the beach at the edge of the track, but nothing else was there. The beach was deserted, as far as the eye could see in either direction, and the horizon was bare of ships. There was nothing but palm trees, and a votive cross. Why, I wondered, was that there? For the fishermen? Or had some Portuguese caravel come to grief there years ago? There was a crudely-planked fishing boat that showed evidence of long disuse. I rested my motorcycle against a palm trunk, for the sand was too soft to use its stand, took off my clothes, hung them on the handlebars, and walked into the sea. I swam out to look back at the coast, the foreshore and the distant low hills, and wondered why the Portuguese had never pushed inland. Too difficult? Were the people there less than welcoming? Or had Goa served its purpose adequately, and the Portuguese commercial avarice satisfied by their chain of trading stations running entirely round Africa, to India, to Malaya, and on to the coast of China at Macao? For a relatively small nation, it was no small enterprise. But my thinking came to an end.

As I turned back to the beach, to my dismay I saw a man carrying coconuts walk out of the palms, pause at my motorcycle to look for its owner, and make his way on to the sand. Similarly, out of nowhere, he was joined by a girl selling bangles and necklaces. The beach vendors swarm at places like Colva, but here? Why here? There couldn't have been another tourist for two miles in either direction. Maybe even further. There are limits to how long, even if you needed to cool off, you want to continue the process. After another twenty minutes I was in near-manic desperation to do anything rather than continue paddling around, as if I were training to swim to Mombasa.

Have you ever tried persuading an Indian beach vendor that you don't want a coconut, or a drink of coconut milk, or a bangle, or a mirror bag, when you are treading water stark naked twenty-five yards offshore, and they, becoming more and more voluble, convinced they've hit the jackpot, are at the water's edge? Eventually they turned away, much disappointed, dragging their feet, looking back repeatedly to see if I would change my mind. I waited, giving them time to get well inshore. Nudism Is Prohibited? If Coconuts and Bangles were still lurking, at least I'd given them a fair chance to hike out of sensitivity range. I was alone. I dried in the sun.

I'd expected to see the two vendors at the drinks shack, but they'd vanished. Two British tourists were there, their rental mopeds parked outside. Neither Ken nor Julie was enjoying India.

"She didn't like Delhi. She nearly cried. And we didn't like Agra, did we, there's nothing to see there but the Taj. The streets were terrible, all the people, and the dirt, and the animals."

"We were taken to see a carpet factory. They had all these little boys and women working because their fingers are small . . ."

"Nimble" said Ken.

"Yes, nimble, and they were singing this song as they worked. He told us, didn't he Ken? They were singing they wished happiness to everyone who would walk on the carpet."

Ken switched to local matters. "What do you think about Colva then? It's not much, is it? Bit of a mess really. And you should see our toilet."

"It's just a hole in the ground. We decided to go to Goa to see if it was better. We didn't want to see any more of India, not if it was all like that, like Agra." Julie sounded disappointed.

Ken went for another round of fizzy soft drinks and returned saying "We've been here three weeks and we're going to move on now, aren't we? Delhi, we'll fly back there because we've got to, but then we're going to Bangkok, Singapore, Hong Kong, Australia, New Zealand, Tokyo, Honolulu, LA, Toronto, New York and then home, aren't we?" The list of destinations, heard in a Goan beach shack, sounded like something out of the Arabian Nights. Travel to regions beyond belief.

Julie was still on her carpet back in Agra.

"They cost so much. Even a little one was £400. I had one once, a pink one, which belonged to my Grand'mum. I don't know where she got it from. She must have had it shipped from India. It was pink-like and I suppose it was for a bedroom, but we had it in the living room and then it got a bit frayed, so we gave it away. I wish I hadn't now. I'd no idea what they cost. If I'd known that, we could have got it repaired. Now I don't think we can afford to get one."

"Not on our budget." said Ken.

I had thought of going to the north coast of Goa and trying that, but suddenly, like Ken and Julie, I was at the end of my visit to India. Going back to my hotel I passed its nearest rival and there, sitting in a circle of cane chairs on the sand and weed that passed as a front lawn, was a group of six tourists, the sexes evenly divided, with their guru. His disciples, eyes tightly closed, were taut with the concentration of relaxing and his eyes flicked snakelike from one to the other, gauging their tolerance of his overlordship. Then, sensing the spell could not hold much longer, he "woke" them and prompted them into singing a mantra; and their voices, hesitant, embarrassed, fought for air space with the shouts of the Kingfisher drinkers rallying at the beach bar for their sundowners.

Think about Goa and you think about the Costa Brava, the Costa del Sol, the Famagusta coast, Ayia Napa and Nissi Beach, or Mombasa, with Malindi and Diani. The list could go on. We've all been to the original sun, sea, and sand paradises. Has Goa sold its soul? Yes, but maybe not. If I appear to have been tough on Goa, it is not so. My target has been my own kind; and by my own choice I kept away from the star resorts, the success stories in the Goan tourist boom. The Colvas can be contained, and can, in time, be transformed. At the end of the day, is it not economics, rather than aesthetics or conservancy, that normally calls the shots?

My final stop in India was Bombay, the Mumbai of today, and then, like Ken and Julie, it was home. That one last port of call, compared to Central India, might well prove to be terminal shock, even after Goa. I had been to Bombay before, but had always been passing through, bound elsewhere. This time, for a few days at least, I would stay there.

Twelve

The New Go-Getters

 Why, I wondered, was it that the Indian Airlines Airbuses just brought into service already looked as if they were ten years old? The fuselage and wings were stained with oil, inside the cabin the bulkheads were dirty and the seats worn and torn, as indeed they are on the Golden Triangle's high profile Delhi–Agra Shatabdi Express. It hardly builds up passenger confidence, but you get accustomed, anesthetized, if you like, to the negative aspects of travel in India.

If you are to preserve your mental equilibrium the first, basic, Golden Rule in your travelling is to reduce the stress factor. Whatever happens, roll with it. Accept delays as inevitable. Five-hour delays are normal if you travel by air. Be pleasantly surprised if you take off within that five-hour period, or (it can happen) on time. The follow-on rule is never travel with more luggage than you can look after yourself, even in this land of porters and would-be carriers of every piece of baggage you have. Even better, if you're flying, restrict yourself to what you can carry on. Don't check anything. It's not that it will be stolen or lost; it's just that it may take forever to claim your bags at your destination.

Porters or not, you will want wads of notes in small denominations, for the need for tips is endless. The continual disbursement of petty cash is not so much the essential lubricant that keeps India going, but installments paid on the insurance policy that safeguards your living space, preserves your sanity, and allows you to achieve at least half of what you set out to do. You must be patient. You must expect that it will take twenty minutes or more to sign a credit card voucher, or to pay a hotel bill. You must expect staggering, pedantic bureaucracy, papers in quintuplicate, such a confusion of management that you are reduced to near-hysteria in a bank or a post office. Ride along with it, together with the crowd. For you are rarely alone, and as you go about your Main Street business you will be pushed, shoved, blocked, and carried along in a tide of your fellow human beings, none of whom has street manners as you know them. Most of them will take an unsolicited and intimate interest in everything you are doing, or trying to do. Respond. Try smiling. Talk to them. You may get tired of the 40-watt bulbs, the brain-damaging pollution of two-stroke engines, the badly tuned taxis, and the diesel-belching trucks and buses, but live with it. You are fortunate to have the electricity, and the powered transport. Many don't.

In India even the poorest man, woman, and child will wash himself or herself scrupulously each day, but the standard of environmental cleanliness in India is lower than in Africa, lower than in South America, lower than in Southeast Asia. You must be prepared to find litter and human excrement everywhere, be it city garden, village field, or road verge. Be prepared to find fountains that don't work, ponds that are fouled, and hopelessly contaminated water sources. Does the threat of cholera surprise you? Get all your shots before you travel. Typhoid, tetanus, polio, cholera, meningitis, hepatitis, and rabies. You need your chloroquine or Paludrine and Fansidar for malaria, and your mosquito repellent. You need Steritabs for your drinking water. You need Immodium and Dioralyte for when it all goes wrong, and it's no bad idea to take acidolphilus pills daily, which boost lactobacillus acidophilus cultures in your body so that you can assimilate Indian food without it acting like a bacterial depth charge in your lower regions. Since you are already carrying a staggering weight of medicines you might as well add a course of antibiotics, and some vitamins before you set out. The current United Nations projection is that south-central Asia (that's Afghanistan, Pakistan, India, and Bangladesh) will more than double its current population of 1.5 billion by the middle of this century. The environmental and health aspects of this staggering increase are the most serious threat, other than another war with Pakistan, facing India at this time.

Despite my health warnings, once I cut away from the tourist circuit, I eat only Indian food. I eat at roadside dhabas and live on chapattis, nan, samosas, and tikis, using a mohba leaf as a bowl and fingers as eating irons. Two can eat well for six rupees. In a hotel much the same will cost sixty rupees each and the food will probably be more suspect in terms of hygiene, for roadside food is cooked for you then and there. In the international hotels, however, you are relatively safe. Against all inbred instincts, if you play it the Indian way, you will survive. Janet, after Amritsar, does not concur with this approach.

Is survival no more than the passive acceptance of anything that comes your way? Are we back to karma? Not quite. Do your homework; mistrust most timetables, programs, and promises; and plan on the worst case. If you are travelling alone, in other words outside a group tour, allow one day in five simply as a cushion, a shock absorber, and a day in hand. You'll need it. And allow at least half a day per task if you have to buy tickets, send off a parcel, or do anything like that. By the evening of every third day spent in India I have vowed never to return again. But the following morning, in the smoke and smell of the cooking fires, somehow my resolution vanishes and I look forward to the new day. All is forgiven, all is forgotten. I don't know why I have this terrible, irrational, compulsion to see India, to try to understand India, to make some sense of India. It is foolish. It is impossible. India is too old, too great, too complex, too contradictory, and too diverse. The span is too great from the peasant, the simple villager who would have been equally at home in Ashokas's day, to the pilot of my A310 Airbus or the technocrats of India's nuclear missile program.

My companion on the flight to Bombay (now called Mumbai, but I use the name as it was then) was a Hindu businessman who had been born in Lahore. His family had been forced south at Partition, survived the massacres, and arrived in India with nothing but the clothes they stood in. Now head of a company manufacturing newspaper printing presses, he was exporting his presses to Russia and had other export orders stacked up and on hold. His son had just returned from the States with a Boston B.A. to his credit, and was in the business with him.

"Twice the western nations have made it worse in what they call India. They think that all men can be brothers, but it is not like that. The Muslims in Pakistan cannot believe that we are the largest Muslim nation in the world, and here the Muslims are free. They are citizens, they have the same rights as the Hindus, the Sikhs, the Christians, and they can follow their own religion. How is it in Pakistan? Not that way at all. And they make trouble, and I do not think it will end. Twice now we could have ended it, in Kashmir and when we were nearly in Lahore, but the western nations made us stop. So nothing is solved and I do not see that it will end."

I'd long thought that another Indo-Pak war was in the cards, before the weaponry on either side became too lethal and nuclear weapons would be taken as the last resort of the loser. Both sides had military forces that were far too large for comfort, and disarmament, even partial disarmament, seemed out of the question. I knew the figures for Pakistan: foreign debt and military expenditure absorbed two-thirds of the budget, and the slice given the armed services amounted to three times the total sum the government spent on health and education. The figures for India, I guessed, were comparable. But we were moving into another vein.

"If it was not for the mistakes of our government and the bureaucrats, we would be in the top rank of the nations. We can still make it, and we shall, but we have got to get rid of these government people who earn only five thousand rupees (about US$340 or UK£200) and can tell someone from my company or another to get out of their office. It is this power, that is all they have, and there are far too many of them. They do not add anything. The British used to tie up their files with red tape and that is what they left us, this red tape, and we have perfected it."

I asked about the population explosion and whether, at the end of the day, the sheer burden of human numbers would keep Indian initiative in bondage. The answer was impassioned.

"The poor people know nothing and have anything, eight to ten children, even more. The women you see begging have all these children, each ten months apart, you see them on the streets with her, and one at her (he gestured wildly at his chest) and then still another in her tummy. The educated people have no more than two to three children now. No more. But the birth rate, because of these poor people, will go on rising."

We were nearing Bombay and he asked what I was going to do there. I mentioned the museum at Ghandi's house in Laburnum Road. It was a hit.

"My father, who was a prominent Nationalist, took me to see him when I was twenty-one. I tell you he had a face that I cannot describe, there was such power in it, in your religion I would say that it was like the face of Christ. You do not see such a light in the politicians now, but maybe one day we will have someone who will come along like that . . ."

Arriving in Bombay is a shock. It always is. It's the sudden transition to a high-rise city, the curve of the Arabian Sea coastline, the chaos of the traffic, and that great sweep of Back Bay from Malabar to Nariman Point. Strangely, by arriving by sea it's easier to absorb, at least initially, but arriving by air is very different, for driving in from the airport you run the full gamut of the transition from open fields to plate glass. It is a shock. It's the highly visible evidence of another life, posters everywhere advertising consumer goods amongst which JULIET BRAS AND PANTIES were pretty straightforward, and SHEETS YOU CAN PLAN YOUR LIFESTYLE AROUND offered a refreshing approach to the business of living. It's the naked flesh and improbable curves of the heroines of the latest hit movies that bring the Bombay posters to vibrant life. AN EROTIC YOUNG GIRL was rampant jailbait, and the vestigial shredded remains of the uniform worn by JUNGLE JAWAANI (a jawan is a soldier), who looked as if she could teach the erotic young girl a trick or two, was eye-catching to say the least. Lakshmibai, is this your India?

The newsstands reflect the glitz. The magazines *Eve's Weekly*, *Special Star Style*, *Savvy*, and *Debonair*, and their contents reflect the consumer stakes and the angst and hypnotism about sex that seem to come with a rising lifestyle. The captions blaze it:

THE NEW GO-GETTERS. WHAT WILL INDIA'S YOUNG UPWARDLY MOBILE URBAN PEOPLE FIND FULFILLING IN THE 90s? WILL THE YUPPIE TREND CONTINUE?

THE POIGNANT TALE OF A SINGLE PARENT

BEAUTY Q&A FOR KISSABLE LIPS

DR SHETTY, DID YOU RAPE SHEELA ON YOUR EXAMINATION TABLE?

Somehow the sight of an Indian centerfold still comes as a shock, but it wouldn't take long to get absorbed in the world of the racy Maruti Suzukis and the local fast set. Maybe it's better to hit Bombay first and take India second. It would be less of a culture shock, for Bombay is a world apart, a city of ten million with the make-up of Los Angeles (Bombay is the movie capital of the world) and the infrastructure of a mega-Cairo. In population alone it dwarfs every other city in India save for Calcutta, which is perhaps half a million behind. Delhi, in third position, is barely in the league at 4.5 million. But it's not just numbers. It's that lifestyle, or at least the lifestyle of the people who count. Compared to them, Calcutta could be on another planet.

I was staying in high-rise luxury with the head of a foreign bank and his wife. Possibly as a vaccination against the potentially spoiling effect of their rarefied and protected environment, she had become more and more involved with charity work. A year down the road she had taken as her particular concern the Garden School established by Sister Felicity Morris of the Order of Jesus and Mary at 15 Nathalal Parekh Marg. Did I want to go there? She had a visit to make. The answer was yes, without any hesitation.

The school's low buildings flank a playground square and the setting is far removed from the slums from which the children have come. We were taken around by Mother Felicity, and as we went from classroom to classroom there was nothing remarkable to see but small children in uniform bent at their desks, their attention almost wholly directed to the lesson in hand with the odd, stray mischievous glance to see who their visitors were. At break there was an explosion of children into the playground and the noise and laughter could have been that of a schoolyard anywhere. About thirty children a year are taken into the school from the streets and the slums, all of them without any hope, any education, any future. They are taught primarily in English and brought to the standard of education that permits them to be placed in the Indian school system at the age of fourteen on an equal footing with any child.

Just over a hundred children attend the school. It is entirely dependent on charity and the cost per child per year works out at about 1,200 rupees (about $85, or £50). Ten thousand rupees (rounded up roughly $700, or £410) would cover the cost of a child through the entire course. Surrounded by these children writing in their exercise books with such painstaking concern, you realize the human potential that is run to waste in poverty. There's nothing remarkable in that thought, I know, but then you wonder what happens later. What will these children do when they leave school? Can any society with an explosive growth rate ever hope to achieve a state in which every child has an equal start and equal opportunity? Question leads to question, and there are no answers except, as Mother Felicity is doing, to work to a certain end in a small way and, I would guess, be content that you are blessed with success in what you have started.

"We want educational toys, but do not send us." she told me as we walked to the gate of the playground. "It is money, I'm afraid. We must have money, not gifts, for the Customs open everything. They will steal what you send to sell themselves, put an Indian toy in its place and wrap the parcel again. It is a dreadful thing to say about my own country, but it is true."

For me the visit was a timely reminder that the glitter of Malabar Hill, Marine Drive, and Colaba is as substantial as tinsel. I'm not suggesting that we should all adopt sackcloth and ashes to purge our hang-ups, if we have them, about being favored by fortune from birth, but it's no bad thing every now and again to be reminded "There, but for the Grace of God . . ." If you want to see the kind of places these children came from, go to Dharvari, 60 Feet Road, somewhere like that, but I don't think it's necessary, and a deliberate visit made just to rubberneck at human misery would be a gross intrusion into their unsought deprivation.

I made one last visit before I left Bombay, not back to Mother Felicity, nor to the slums, but to the Bombay Hospital in Sir Vithaldas Thackersey Marg. I needed background for a novel I had started to sketch out, and there, bent over my notebook, I was startled to be called by name. An Indian whose face was familiar came towards me, but I couldn't place him. Then suddenly, with a convulsive mental leap backwards light years in time to what was already another existence, I had it: he had been a compartment companion on our train journey from Amritsar to Delhi. We had parted in Delhi. The chances of such a meeting, in another city, weeks later, quite apart from factoring in the population of India, were odds that could never be expressed, save as a decimal point preceeded by many zeros.

The next night I was flying out, to return home. My flight was delayed, and I spent an hour reading The *Times of India* from front page to the classifieds. The domestic news was disturbing. The incidence of crime directed against tourists, from hotel room robbery to street hold-ups, was rising to unprecedented levels; but then so was tourism hitting new highs. Our departure time was put back another hour. By then, every scrap of domestic and international news exhausted, I turned to the matrimonial columns. I had thought that arranged marriages were slowly becoming a part of the past. Not so, it seemed. The lists go on covering entire pages under the headings "Wanted Brides" and "Wanted Grooms."

> **ALLIANCE invited from good looking fair complexioned home loving cultured girls for handsome Kutchi Brahmin boy 32 Electronic Engineer having own established manufacturing business with three factories and ownership flat at Andheri Bombay widely traveled in Europe and Far East on business tours, selection based on meretorial credentials rather than caste community or horoscope. Apply Box XXXX.**

The style and language of the matrimonial ads were much the same. For the man, hardly surprisingly, education, profession, and assets counted. For the girl, it was looks: "slim," "fair," "beautiful," "tall," "wheatish," and a hint of domestic qualities. "Homely" and "home loving" featured far more often than education and career, and "convent educated" seemed to be a definite plus in a matrimonial resumé.

Mother Felicity's girls might yet find an India of equal opportunity ready for them, for in the advertisements, time and time again, caste was stated to be of no importance.

❖ ◆ ❖

There's that moment as you fasten your seat belt when you feel like a deflated balloon. Temporarily you're going nowhere, save where you will be taken. There's no need for the energy, the dynamism, which has kept you going up to that point, and as the aircraft doors close, that sense of limbo is reinforced. You are no longer part of the world you're leaving. You are committed to the world of your destination. Suddenly I felt as if I'd been away from it for half a lifetime.

I rarely sleep on a long-haul flight. We headed to London's Heathrow Airport carrying the light of the rising sun with us. Perhaps unable to face new realities so immediately, my memory switched back; and I escaped into a dream world.

Dreams and Reality

Thirteen

Nagada. An Indian Reverie

Rajasthan. Udaipur

"Jagniwas is the Lake Palace island, about 1.5 hectares in size. The palace was built by Maharana Jagat Singh II in 1754 and covers the entire island. Today it has been converted into a luxury hotel with courtyards, fountains, gardens, and a swimming pool. It's a delightful place, and even if you can only dream of staying there, it's worth the trip out to have a look around . . . "

India. Lonely Planet.

I go back in time to an early visit to India in 1984. I know of no reason why travel should not be sybaritic. My travels, all too often, seem to have pursued the reverse track, and Janet, while often expressing lively and uncensored comment on the turn of events, has stayed with me.

For once, unashamedly, we would find the equivalent of a Moghul garden of delight. The Lake Palace has two premier suites: the Kush Mahal, which faces east, towards the city palace and the city, and the Sajjan Niwas, which faces west, over the lake and the hills, towards the ridgeline where the sun will set. Libran to a fault, I couldn't make up my mind which one to take, so I booked each one, in turn, over two successive nights. I'd told Janet that we'd take a break from our planned itinerary and go to Udaipur for two days, but no more than that.

As we landed at the small airport the early morning sun rose into the sky, shimmering red in its own heat haze, the colors of a Rajasthan dawn were violent, though muted: deep reds, purple, and volcanic black. The sun turned from red to yellow and then incandescant as we passed through a series of broken hills, curving down towards the Ahar River valley, Lake Pichola, and Udaipur. Within minutes it seemed the sun had burnt the land beyond redemption to a uniform desert tan. No, wrong word. Read that as khaki. Of course the Indian word was the right word. The landscape was an apparent near total desolation of rocky hillsides and dry river beds, with a few struggling trees and sparse vegetation. The villages, and the hard-won fields around them, were all the more surprising. A sign nailed to a tree outside one subsistence-level village spelled out the rules of survival:

TREE MEANS WATER
WATER MEANS BREAD
BREAD MEANS LIFE

A brilliant flash of glowing crimson. By the village well a woman in a deep flame-colored sari was carrying two gleaming brass water pots on her head. It fitted. It was right. Color such as that showed vibrant life.

Our driver braked without warning as a bird about the size of a pheasant broke out of some bushes just in front of us at windshield level, its frantic wings beating to gain vital height, trailing a stream of iridescent green and indigo feathers.

Janet was delighted. "A wild peacock. Did you see it? Did you see it?"

Udaipur was a bewildering mass of sensations, crowded streets, some modern villas, a city wall, and then a town that looked more Greek than Indian, flat-roofed white- and ochre-painted houses piled on houses, a turquoise window frame, narrow streets, steps, balconies, wood shutters, and small shops. Then a mixture of more high walls, the glimpse of an extravagant, towering palace, tiered like a giant wedding cake, a great fortress gateway, a garden, and we were winding down a steep hill. I asked Janet to close her eyes as our taxi made the descent to the landing stage on the Bhansi Ghat, by the edge of Lake Pichola.

"Trust me now. Don't open your eyes until I say so." I guided her to the edge of the dock and made her stand so that she was facing out across the lake.

"Now!"

She stood spellbound. The Lake Palace was in front of us, radiant white in the early sunlight, long, low, apparently floating on the mirror smooth waters of the lake like a fantastic marble pleasure boat, an image doubled by its reflection in the morning calm.

"Your house for two days. Do you think it'll be all right?"

She kept squeezing my hand, unable to speak.

Later, in the boat, I broke into her silent enchantment. "I'm going to make you do it again."

"What?"

"Close your eyes. When we've booked in. You'll see. Or rather, you won't. Not until I tell you to look. There's one small surprise to come."

"There can't be. It's just fabulous. I've always wanted to stay here. I never dreamt we could. Isn't it desperately expensive? I wonder what the rooms are like. They must have fabulous views."

My reply was deliberately low key. "It'll be OK, I think."

"Welcome to the Lake Palace. The Sajjan Niwas suite is yours, as you requested. If you would sign here, and here is your key, which the bearer will take and he will guide you. Your suitcases will come directly. We hope you will enjoy your stay."

I made Janet stand outside the door of the room after we'd climbed the short staircase to our floor.

"Just stay here. Until I come for you."

I went in to get my own bearings in unknown territory, and came out again almost at once, thanking and dismissing our guide.

"Now close your eyes." She did as she was told. I led her into the room, and then around to the left. She told me later that she'd had a feeling that

137

we'd moved from one room to another. We halted shortly after we entered the second room.

"Now open them."

She gasped. We were in a bedroom. The light was greenish from the paintings on the walls, trees, flowers, two nautch girls, reflected and re-reflected in great mirrors. A swing with a silk cushion hung from gilded links from the ceiling, and on the ceiling, above the beds, was another mirror. It was fantastic. A doorway appeared to lead into a bathroom beyond the bedroom, and windows, deep carved embrasures, large enough for two, piled with silk cushions and bolsters, looked out over the lake.

"Shall we go on?"

The bathroom was plain white marble. We didn't linger there. We passed through the green glow of our exotic bedroom into the first room we'd entered. It was a great reception room, filled with Victorian furniture, heavy, almost grotesque, and yet somehow entirely fitting in that setting. Great paintings were on the walls, and the center of the room was dominated by one tremendous, quite hideous, chandelier.

"It's fantastic. I shall never leave here. I don't want to go anywhere else."

"You haven't seen it all yet." I led her out on to a wide roof terrace overlooking half the lake and the distant hills. On the other side there was a small courtyard beneath us, and, far beyond the roofs of the hotel, the town of Udaipur with the massive walls of the City Palace plunging down to the waters of the lake.

"I will, you know. I'll never leave. You shouldn't have brought me here." Janet had been thinking. "That was a pretty quick guided tour you gave yourself while I was waiting outside. How could you learn about everything in that length of time?"

"I didn't. It wasn't necessary."

"Why not?"

"I used to live here. When I was the Maharana Sajjan Singh. These apartments were my pleasure house. I came here with my dancing girls. You are but the last of a long line, but quite the loveliest of them all. I shall keep you here, bathed in scented water, perfumed in oil, until the sherbet is finished and the last musician has laid down his instrument, exhausted."

Two hours later we were in another taxi. It took us little more than half an hour to reach Nagada. We turned off the main road about a kilometer before Eklingi, and drove skirting the lake on a dirt road before reaching the temple site. Our driver turned his car around and sought the shade of some nearby trees. It was close to noon. We were quite alone. No one else was there. The sun struck diamonds of light off the water. In hard black silhouette against the brilliance of the water there was a small temple in the lake, its foundations submerged, just columns and roof showing. On the shoreline were two other small temples. We walked slowly towards them, the heat of the day caught and magnified by the low bowl of hills.

"I don't know who built these temples. All I know is that they're old. I don't even know how I heard about them, but I knew we had to come here. One might have been my temple. One might well have been yours. They're called the Mother and Daughter-in-Law, so maybe that counts me out. But were you that daughter?"

We wandered around the platform surrounding the temple structures, and then went inside the sanctuary of the larger temple into the shade. Everything was still. There was no sound, no movement. With a curiously heightened sensitivity to our surroundings we went outside again. There, by the edge of the temple platform, was a smooth grey upright stone standing proud by itself, round-ended and capped with marigolds. It had petals around its base.

"The flowers are fresh. Someone must have put them there today."

"What is it?"

"A lingam. It's the symbol of Shiva, the reproducer. He has a bad side too as the destroyer, but I think we're dealing with sex rather than destruction here. His mate was Parvati, the beautiful. Perhaps we'll find her in the little temple."

We walked on to the smaller temple and started looking at the carvings, done in small votive groups, on the outside. Janet's eye was caught by a sinuous wave of motion. She drew her breath in sharply as a snake disappeared into a crack in the temple wall. Then she drew in her breath a second time. Close to where the snake had been was a shingara scuplture, a small carved group of six figures. Flanked by two high-breasted attendants of her own sex, a central female figure was bent over, her bared breasts pendant, in front of three males. One was taking her from the rear. She steadied herself, hand above the knee of another, while she took his penis in her mouth. The third, apparently discomfited by her wanton display, had covered his eyes with his hands. Without conscious direction we found ourselves back inside the first, larger, sanctuary. Janet came into my arms. Over her shoulder I could see the gateway outside the stone flagged entry, the lake, and the bare hillside beyond. All the colors were washed out in the blaze of noon.

"No?"

"Not now. With darkness and fires outside, dancing, and garlands of flowers, perhaps, and the throbbing of drums. You would need handmaidens, and you have none." I led her back into the blinding daylight.

We reached the Lake Palace Hotel at lunchtime. On our way past the desk I arranged for a boat to take us to Jag Mandir, the sister island to our own, late that afternoon.

There were eight of us, excluding the boatman, in the launch leaving for Jag Mandir. To our relief, when we landed on the little island, the boatman stayed with his craft. There was no one to guide us. The other couples wandered off, a loose group, bent on exploring the ruined palace. We entered the main building and climbed out on to a flat roof overlooking the whole palace. It was simple in layout, no more than three sides of a great forecourt, but it was exotic for all its apparent simplicity. There were cupolas supported on slender columns, crenellations and fretwork, bougainvillea and roses growing wild. We sat together, looking at it all. In the light of the setting sun the distant hills, ridgeline after ridgeline of sepia tints, looked like a painted backdrop.

"When you are rich, very rich, will you buy this place for me?"

"Of course."

"I love it. I love our palace too, but I love this one the most. I'm sure I've lived here before. I have. Haven't I?"

"You might have come here with Shah Jehan. He took refuge here about four hundred years ago after unwisely challenging Jahangir, his father. Shah Jehan was the one who built the Taj Mahal. They say he got some of his ideas from this place. But I don't think you were here with him. He was crazy about Mumtaz, the wife for whom he built the Taj."

"I know I wasn't Mumtaz."

"Then it must have been another time. Perhaps you were British, not Indian at all. In 1857 all the refugees from this part of Rajasthan took shelter here."

"But I don't feel Victorian. I think I feel more like Parvati."

We called room service and ordered drinks when we got back. The sun was setting, a full circle of intense white-yellow light nearly touching the top of the brown hills. The horizon above the most distant ridge flared with orange. Drinks in hand on our terrace, we watched the fire of the disc vanish, almost as if it had been wound down into the center of the earth. The surface of the lake shivered in the afterglow, patterned in ripples as if the going down of the sun had caused a sudden chill. But there was no wind. The evening temperature was unchanged.

"Tomorrow we'll see Udaipur. The City Palace. And then shall we try to find a place where you can buy a dancing girl outfit? Let's have another drink. Then we'll go down and eat?" I took her glass.

"No, let's have supper here." There was a sudden urgent enthusiasm in the request. "Order now. Get them to leave it set out so that it stays warm, and then we can eat when we want."

"Why don't we go downstairs? Wouldn't it be easier?"

"No. I want to have a bath. And I don't want to go down to a dining room."

I stayed on the terrace. The last of the afterglow had given way to the horizon blue of early night.

"Please may I have my drink now?"

I hardly heard her, but something unusual about Janet's fleeting silhouette in the doorway arrested my attention. The night air stirred: it was no more than a cat's-paw, a momentary caress of warm wind, but in it was a waft of fragrance, attar, musk, balm, and the promise of all the flowers of Shalimar.

The "Shalimar" brought into my mind was the Shalimar Garden three miles east of Lahore on the Grand Trunk Road, where Janet and I had taken the four-month-old Victoria in 1968, only to be disappointed at its state of dilapidation at that time.

It was built by Shah Jehan, the builder of the Taj Mahal, for his court including, of course, his much-loved Mumtaz. It was a garden of delight. Essentially three terraces in a walled garden with white marble royal apartments and pavilions and gardens, it was bisected by watercourses and fountains. Between paired staircases leading to the lowest terrace, multiple rows of small recesses had been pigeon-holed into the marble wall behind the central channel waterfall. These shallow alcoves held lamps at night, which showed as myriad points of light, turning the fall into a shimmering silver curtain. The term "Shalimar" has been brand-named to this effect, rarely but sometimes employed as a decorative technique to this day. It was here, at night, by moonlight, that the dancing girls played for Shah Jehan.

Fourteen

War Elephants. The Fears of the Small Hours of the Night

 Why do we travel? Surely the answer is simple? Curiosity. To cross the river to see what it's like on the other bank. To go over a mountain pass to check out the next valley. To visit a known destination because you've heard about it. How do you travel? In a group, like Chaucer's band of pilgrims? Alone? Let's close the ring. Do you know where you're going? Do you know where you are staying each night? There are so many parameters. We are all different, and we take our lives in different ways, but there is perhaps one common factor. Unless you are a war journalist, a soldier of fortune, or a mercenary for hire, generally safety, your safety, is the prime consideration.

Would I travel now in Afghanistan and Pakistan as we did, with Janet in her sixth and eighth months of pregnancy, and a child under two? The answer is obvious. "No." Would I travel in the region at all now? Not in Afghanistan, nor Pakistan, nor Kashmir. In Southern India, yes. But you have to ask yourself, do I need to go there now? How long will it be before any of us feel free to roam as we wish, if indeed you feel comfortable travelling the way we did.

I do not suffer from insomnia, but in 2002 I found myself waking in the small hours of the night acutely concerned about the future of the region about which I was writing. Having set out into what was then unfamiliar territory, and come to know a little of it, it's not possible to return home, close your door, and forget it. At least not for me. There are people like you and me out there. Not strangers. Not aliens. Their cares and concerns are the same as ours. At this time we have taken into our hands the power to shape events in their world. Are we on the right course?

I used the word "course." As a sailor, perhaps a marine analogy is valid. I would not set out on a route I had not taken before, or for a strange coast, without reading every source I could find about it. A great deal of homework necessarily precedes any passage, unless you're set on reinventing the wheel and recalculating the calendar. You also find, sailing in constricted waters or a narrow marked channel, that looking behind you is as important as looking ahead, for otherwise you will veer off course. You can try just looking ahead, but it's about as safe as removing the rearview mirrors from your car.

Afghanistan is in a far graver state than Germany was in 1945. It is hemorrhaging, not recovering, even though Taliban dominance has been broken. After decades of conflict and ruinous damage, given the ancient tribal and linguistic divisions, let alone its divisive geography, the Afghans cannot pull themselves up by their own bootstraps. For Afghanistan it is as if the entire United States, or the whole of Europe, had its government buildings, cathedrals, churches, museums, monuments, historic sites, and cities leveled, communication systems, generating plants, power lines, and fuel supplies destroyed, irrigation channels ruined, airports and roads cratered. Road verges, fields, playgrounds, and the land around any area, inhabited or uninhabited, once reckoned to be a war target or vital ground, are now unmarked killing zones, sewn with mines and unexploded cluster bombs. Not one week passes without the consequential death or traumatic injury of some hapless adult or child, trying to go about his or her normal business, trying to resume a normal life. When I make my comparison, I know the scale is different on all counts. But my image is valid.

Above this, Afghanistan's tangible cultural past has been pounded into ruins, and an infrastructure, which had struggled to hold a shattered country together, no longer exists. It is hardly surprising that the result, seen objectively in the Islamic world, is shock, horror, and bitterness. It will take more than a century for Afghanistan to recover, even given massive post-war aid. It will take four to five generations before the bitterness and the memory of this time of horror will fade; and five hundred years before it is "history." Afghanistan has suffered the invasion of many conquerors over the last three thousand years. The worst, like Jahansoz the World Burner, and the Russians, left ruins behind them. The best, like Alexander the Great, and the Moghul Emperors, built cities, pleasure gardens, public buildings, observatories, schools, bazaars, roads, irrigation systems, and won, in their time, peace and happiness. Afghanistan desperately needs an equivalent of the 1945 Marshall Plan. I see no evidence of it. As I was writing this book, the fears of nuclear war between Pakistan and India, the Israeli–Palestinian conflict, and the clear indications that the US Administration had already decided to storm and subjugate Iraq, probably early in 2003, totally eclipsed the resolution of Afghanistan's problems.

If Afghanistan relapses into civil war and tribalism, it will affect Pakistan. If Pakistan catches a new wave of Islamic insurrection, the terrorist groups in Kashmir will not be restrained. Already the United States is in the extraordinary position of supporting a dictatorship in which the life, liberty, and pursuit of happiness of its citizens is no more advanced than in the Dark Ages, facing off against the only democracy in the region. What if India goes to war with Pakistan for the fourth time? Pakistan has lost each war, and over the last fifty years a national psyche has developed in which they see themselves outnumbered, beleaguered, and pinned in a narrow fertile strip of land with their backs against a mountain wall. Would they resort to nuclear weapons? A mindset exists in Pakistan that might well trigger that reaction. As Semiramis knew before she challenged India, they had war elephants. Today those elephants are still there, but they have tusks with nuclear tips. I have no doubt, as Semiramis found to her cost, they would be used. For the United States the vital issues of today are peace in the region and peace in the Middle East. It demands the leadership, perception, and religious tolerance of a second Akbar, and the courage, and selflessness, of Lakshmibai. The subordination of these enduring crises to partisan domestic politics endangers us all, just as the proscription, sentencing, and invasion of target nations could well result in a world divided by religious faith, the like of which has not been seen since the eleventh century.

If, one day, you are in India, go to Jhansi. Sit on the walls of the fort above Lakshmibai's private courtyard, overlooking the city. Find the successor to my old boatman, for someone surely must, by now, have taken his place, and go across the lake; go to her temple. Go to Kalpi, Kotah-ki-Serai, and Gwalior, as I did. Let the past speak. I have a feeling that if India, and the region, is to find a road into the twenty-second century, it will be a woman who will achieve it. Pray, for youth is the only hope for the future, that it will be a young woman. In my prayers I pray too for Afghanistan, Pakistan, and the countries through which I drove on my route from Pakistan to England, for is not the whole of Central Asia, in its human kinship and its common historic links, no less than one world?

Lakshmi, if ever the prayers consecrated by the myriad votive lights of Divali are to be answered, let a new age of peace dawn.

Reference

Timelines

An Abbreviated Chronology

Ancient History

2500–2000 BC	Indus River civilization. Planned cities, drainage, indoor sanitation, agriculture, and the wheel. Writing, statuary, jewelery. Maritime trade with the Persian Gulf and the Near East.
c1000 BC	Attempted invasion of India by Queen Semiramis of Assyria.
326 BC	Afghanistan and India invaded by Alexander the Great. Greek settlements left behind on his return to the Near East.
350–100 BC	Hellenistic (Graeco-Bactrian) civilization. Afghanistan and North West Pakistan.
321–185 BC	Mauryan Empire (Northern India and Baluchistan).
100 BC	Alexandrian Eastern Empire largely dissolved.
185 BC–300 AD	Northern India plagued by successive invasions, through Afghanistan, of Huns, Tartars, and Mongolians.

The Indian Subcontinent During the European Middle Ages

320–600 AD   Gupta Empire.

661–1750   Islamic Umayyad Empire brought the height of Islamic civilization to Herat and Western Afghanistan, and touched the borders of India.

1000–1027   Mahmoud of Ghazni raids India 17 times; but establishes, and endows, Ghazni as a university city and center of learning.

1150   Jahansoz (The World Burner) destroys every city in his path, including Qala Bist.

1193   Qutb-ud-din captures Delhi. The first Muslim bid to establish a state in India.

1193–1338   The Muslim Delhi Sultanate.

1398   Timur the Lame (Tamerlane) raids northern India.

The Moghul Dominance

1498   Vasco da Gama reaches Kerala.

1510   The Portuguese take Goa.

1527–1530   Babur, the first of the six Great Moghul Emperors.

1610–1690   The English set up coastal trading posts in India.

1646–1680   The rise of Maratta power in Central India.

1739   Nadir Shah invades India from Persia and sacks Delhi.

1746–1757   The British and French fight each other and the Indians for Indian territory.

British Expansion in India

1757	Robert Clive defeats the Nawab of Bengal at Plassey and breaks French power in India. Calcutta becomes the base for British expansion.
1803	The British take de facto power in Delhi.
1838–1842	British invasion of Afghanistan (ended in a disastrous retreat from Kabul).
1842–1856	British annexation of successive Indian States: Sind, Gwalior, the Punjab, Jhansi, and Oudh (Lakhnao).
1857–1858	The Indian Mutiny.
1858	Direct rule by Britain imposed over India. The Indian capital is transferred to Calcutta.

The British Raj

1876	Queen Victoria declared Empress of India.
1878–79	Second Anglo-Afghan War.
1893–95	Afghan-British Indian border fixed, which splits Pashtun tribal territory, with half in Afghanistan and half in British India (later Pakistan).
1911	King George V's Coronation Durbar in Delhi. The Indian capital is transferred back to Delhi.
1914–1918	The First World War.
1919	Third Afghan-British War. The British formally cede all interest in Afghanistan. The Amritsar massacre in India.
1923–29	Amanullah Khan fails to modernize Afghanistan.

1930	Mahatma Ghandi's protest Salt March in India.
1933	Mohammed Zahir Shah declared king of Afghanistan.
1936	Afghanistan signs a trade agreement with the USSR and a friendship pact with the US.
1939–45	The Second World War.

Independence

1942–1946	The move for Indian Independence led by Mahatma Ghandi gathers momentum. A move to secure a separate Muslim State promoted by Mohammed Ali Jinnah (later the first President of Pakistan).
1947	The northwest and northeastern provinces of India are taken to form Pakistan (with two wings, East and West). India and Pakistan are declared independent nations. Widespread rioting and killing. Half a million deaths and eleven million are homeless in the upheaval.
1947–1964	Jawaharlal Nehru India's first Prime Minister.
1948	Mahatma Ghandi assassinated. The first Indo-Pakistan War (Hyderabad and the Kashmir dispute).

The Descent into Chaos

1953	Afghanistan turns to Russia for economic and military aid after being turned down by the USA.
1956	Pakistan declares itself to be an Islamic Republic.
1961	India reclaims Goa.
1964	Mohammed Zahir Shah deposed as King of Afghanistan. An Afghan Republic is declared.

1965	Indo-Pakistan War (the Rann of Kuch-Sind border in April–June, and Kashmir in September).
1996–1977	Indira Ghandi became Prime Minister of India.
1969	Martial law declared in Pakistan.
1971	Indo-Pakistan War. Weeks of fighting on the West Pakistan border end with Pakistan surrendering. East Pakistan secedes and becomes Bangladesh.
1973	Afghanistan declared an Islamic Republic.
1975	India and Pakistan race to develop nuclear weapons.
1977	Military coup in Pakistan.
1979	Soviet Russia invades and occupies Afghanistan. The former Prime Minister of Pakistan, Zulfikar Ali Bhutto, is executed.
1980	Afghan mujaheddin resistance fighters are funded and armed by Pakistan, the US, and Saudi Arabia, as well as Iran, Egypt, and China.
1984	Indian Army ordered to storm the Golden Temple in Amritsar. Indira Ghandi assassinated by her Sikh guards. Her son Rajiv Ghandi elected Prime Minister.
1988	USSR, Afghanistan, Pakistan, and the US sign an Afghanistan peace treaty. The Soviet army withdraws.
1988–96	Civil war in Afghanistan. The US stands back. Over six million refugees flood into Pakistan. Pakistan supports the fundamentalist Islamic Taliban.
1996	The Taliban capture Kabul. War casualties in Afghanistan from resistance fighting during the Soviet occupation, and the ensuing civil war total 1.9 million killed with 67 percent of these civilian victims.

Immediate Past History

1998	The US strikes at Al Qaeda camps in Afghanistan in retaliation for the terrorist attacks on US embassies in East Africa.
1998	India and Pakistan conduct nuclear weapons tests.
1999	Indo-Pakistan repeated clashes in Kashmir.
1999	UN imposes an embargo on all trade and economic support for the Taliban.
2001	Three weeks after the September 11 terrorist attacks on US targets, the US mounts massive air strikes against Afghanistan. The ground war starts soon after, fought by US air power and Afghan ground forces, primarily Tajik, aided by US and UK special forces.
2002	By the middle of the year it is clear that the Taliban is broken, and Al Qaeda, in Afghanistan, no longer exists as a cohesive force.

Afghanistan, after over twenty years of war, was devastated, and was in danger of relapsing into the chaos of tribal rivalry again unless peace was secured by a sizeable external peace-keeping force, with concurrent civil reconstruction on a massive scale. The Kashmir dispute, fomented by Pakistan-supported terrorist insurgents, brought India and Pakistan to the brink of nuclear conflict. Pakistan, with a military dictatorship that was fast losing credibility, faced internal threats from its own Islamic fundamentalists, as well as insurgent refugees from Afghanistan. India suffered its worst sectarian rioting in years, instigated by Hindu extremists.

If ever there were a time for the intervention of benevolent World Power, exercising all the strength and resources of the United Nations in the interests of peace, it was at this time.

A Capsule Overview of the Indian Mutiny

The First Year. 1857

April	After three months of growing unrest, native soldiers mutiny in Meerut.
May	The insurrection spreads to Delhi. Ten other garrisons and a number of smaller stations are taken by rebels.
June	The revolt spreads to twenty-three other garrisons including Jhansi, Cawnpore (Kanpur), and Lucknow (Lakhnao).
July	A further eight places fall into rebel hands, including Agra where the surviving Europeans take refuge in the Red Fort. A relieving force reaches Cawnpore (Kanpur) the day after captive women and children are murdered.
August	The revolt spreads to five other areas. Mutinies break in Bombay and Madras.
September	Disturbances spread in Northern India. A mutiny is prevented in Karachi. Delhi is recaptured, Bahadur Shah, the King, is taken prisoner, and his sons shot. The relief of Lucknow (Lakhnao) fails.
October	The unrest spreads into Bihar, north Bengal, and Assam. A mutiny in Bombay is forestalled. The refugees in the Red Fort in Agra are rescued.
November	Lucknow (Lakhnao) is relieved. The Residency is evacuated and left abandoned. Near Cawnpore (Kanpur) a British force is defeated by a rebel army.

| December | The British win a decisive victory outside Cawnpore (Kanpur) over Tantya Tope and Rao Sahib. The fortunes of the British are in the ascendant. |

The Second Year. 1858

January	A force sets out to recapture Lucknow (Lakhnao). Sir Hugh Rose sets out with another force for Central India.
March	Lucknow (Lakhnao) is recaptured.
April	Jhansi is stormed and captured: the Rani escapes. Rose goes on to Kalpi.
May	Kalpi is taken. Tantya Tope and the Rani of Jhansi reach Gwalior.
June	Rose reaches Gwalior. The Rani of Jhansi is killed in action. Gwalior is recaptured. The rebels turn to guerrilla warfare in Northern India, and along the Nepalese border.
July–October	The rebel forces are gradually mopped up. Tantya Tope continues active resistance in Central India.
November	Direct rule is imposed over India by Britain.

The Third Year. 1859

In January Bahadur Shah was tried for treason. He refused to answer to the charges. On March 29 he was found guilty, and exiled to Burma. He was 83 years old then; he died in Rangoon on 7 November 1862. Tantya Tope was betrayed and captured by the British on April 7. He was tried on April 15 and executed three days later.

Afternote

Rao Sahib was the last rebel to be captured. He was betrayed in 1862, the year of Bahadur Shah's death. He was hanged.

Principal Indian Rulers and Leaders Featured in This Book

Bajirao II

The Mahratta (Central India) Peshwa or Ruler. Deposed by the British, he was confined to his palace at Bithoor, near Kanpur. He was the father (by adoption) of Nana Saheb, the grandfather of Rao Saheb, and the adoptive "godfather" of Manakarnika (later to become Lakshmibai, Rani of Jhansi), the daughter of his principal adviser. He died in 1851.

Nana Saheb

The adopted son of Bajirao II, and legal heir to the title and lands held by Bajirao II, a succession ruled invalid by the British Administration. He became a leading Indian commander in the revolt against the British in 1858, but was held, probably wrongly, to be the instigator of the uprising in Kanpur in 1857, perhaps because Bithoor was adjacent to Kanpur, or Cawnpore as it was called in British India. Bazaar rumors had it that Nana Saheb crossed into Nepal sometime in 1858 to evade capture and died there, of fever, in 1859. It was never established whether these reports were true.

Rao Saheb

The son of a second son of Bajirao II, Rao Saheb was brought up at Bithoor. He became a leading Indian commander in the revolt against the British in 1858, and was announced as the Peshwa of a resurrected Mahratta Confederacy at a durbar held at Gwalior in 1858. After the defeat of the rebel army at Gwalior he disappeared, rejected the world he had known, and became a mendicant priest. His true identity reported, he was arrested in 1862, taken to Bithoor, and hanged in front of his childhood home.

Lakshmibai, Rani of Jhansi

Born Manakarnika in Varanasi in 1835, she was the daughter of Bajirao II's principal adviser. She lived at Bithoor during her childhood. Nicknamed "Mani," she was considered to be the "goddaughter" of Bajirao II, and at one time was thought to have been earmarked as the bride of Nana Saheb. She was formally married to Gangadhar Rao, the aging Raja of Jhansi, in 1842. On her marriage she took the name of Lakshmibai. The marriage was consummated, on her maturity, in 1851 and later that year she gave birth to a child, who died at three months. Gangadhar Rao, fearing that he might fail to sire a second male child, adopted a five-year-old boy, Damodar Rao, and named him as his heir. On Gangadhar Rao's death in 1853, properly Lakshmibai became the Regent and Ruler of Jhansi for their adopted son. The succession was ruled invalid by the British Administration, and the State of Jhansi taken over.

Lakshmibai was falsely believed to have been responsible for the uprising in Jhansi against the British in 1857. The reverse was true. She sheltered British refugees in the fort until they were taken forcibly by the rebels, which she was powerless to prevent. The following year, realizing that her Jhansi was facing devastion by a British Army of Retribution, she decided to defend the city, and joined Nana Saheb, Rao Saheb, and Tantya Tope in the revolt. Arguably she was the only rebel commander with both instinctive tactical skills and the courage to lead from the front. Her death in action at Kotah-ki-Serai, outside Gwalior, in June 1858 accelerated, and ensured, the inevitable defeat of the rebel army. She was twenty-three years old at her death.

Damodar Rao, although still a child, was held as much to blame as his mother for the 1857 revolt. All Jhansi funds held in trust for him were confiscated, and his title denied.

Tantya Tope

An instructor at the court of Bajirao II in Bithoor. He had at one time been a soldier in the British East Indian Army. He trained both Rao Saheb and Lakshmibai, during their childhood, in riding and martial skills. He joined the revolt in 1857. He was betrayed, and hanged, in 1859.

Glossary

Non-English Words Used in the Text

My use of Urdu, Hindi, and some Pushto words in the text is not to add color, nor an attempt at erudition. There are no English equivalents; or the closest English word carries a slightly different connotation. Karma, to me, is not simply the end result of happenstance; it carries with it predestination linked with inevitability. A nullah is not simply a dry river bed. Many of the words in my list are shared by Hindi and Urdu.

It is the necessary recourse to words like these which, in British India, led to the Anglo-Indian English spoken by British administrators: the British Indian Army, the British regiments serving in India, and bankers, business men, traders, and tea planters across the British Raj. It formed the English spoken in India and Pakistan today. As you travel in these countries you find yourself taking words like these into use, and the definitions and nuances of a different language are absorbed, virtually transdermally, into your vocabulary.

Ayah   A nursemaid, or a lady's maid.

Bagh   A garden.

Bearer   The head male servant in a household, nominally the personal attendant of the male head of the house, charged with responsibility for the male head's clothes, and with waiting upon him and his guests, at table. The military tradition was that your bearer wore

159

your regimental buttons on his tunic, your regimental cummerbund, and your cap badge on his turban.

Begum	A Muslim lady of high status, a matron or older married woman.
Bund	An embankment, normally made around a field to hold water.
Burkha	The black head-to-foot robe worn by Muslim females from the age of puberty onwards always in public and when in front of strangers at home. The eyes alone may be seen. In many cases even the eye slit is netted.
Chadri	The clothing covering the head and shoulders of a Muslim female, which can be drawn across the face to hide all but the eyes. A deference to Islamic tradition that is less severe than a burkha; can be combined with "normal" clothes, and need not be black.
Chaikana	A tea house.
Chappati	Cookie-sized flat round disks of unleavened bread.
Charpoy	A rope-strung bed frame or cot for those who do not want, or cannot afford, box springs.
Chhatri	A cupola-like roof decoration, normally an umbrella dome standing on columns. Also a tomb, or a mausoleum.
Choli	A short-sleeved, close-fitted bodice in Hindu dress.
Chowkidar	A guard or gatekeeper.
Darwaza	A gateway (as in the entry to a city).
Dechi	A round, metal, flat-bottomed cooking pot.
Dhaba	A roadside food stall.

Dhoti	A male waistcloth where the surplus cloth is normally brought forward between the legs and tucked in to the waist.
Diwan	A hall of audience. Diwan i Am that of public audience, Diwan i Khas that of private audience.
Durbar	A formal state ceremony, often linked to a program of events and festivities lasting days, akin to a coronation or a celebration of this magnitude.
Gharri	A horse-drawn seated cart, sometimes used as the word for a taxi.
Ghat	Steps leading down a river bank. Often a cremation place. Also a laundry area (a dhobi ghat).
Guru	A spiritual teacher or sage.
Hartal	A refusal to work. A strike.
Jawan	A male soldier.
Jawaani	A female soldier.
Jezail	A long-barrelled, smooth bore musket, the frontier "rifle" of the pre-rifle firearms age.
Karma	Fate, with predestination and inevitability built in.
Khaki	Desert tan color.
Kwatta	A fort.
Lathi	A long bamboo stick with a lead fill at one end.
Lingam	A phallic stone or symbol (the emblem of the god Siva).
Mahal	A palace.

Maharajah	A prince or the male ruler of an Indian State, sometimes shortened to Rajah, although conventionally the full dignity of the larger states was served by the use of the full name, i.e., "Great King."
Maharani	A princess or the wife of a Maharajah sometimes shortened to Rani.
Mahoot	An elephant trainer, keeper, driver.
Maidan	A central grassed area similar to a village green.
Mali	A gardener.
Mantra	An invocation in the form of a ritual sacred chant, like a hymn, or a prayer.
Masjid	A mosque.
Memsahib	Respectful title used to address someone (always female) in authority.
Mescar	Massacre.
Mihrab	An arched alcove in a mosque pointing towards Mecca.
Mohajir	A Pakistani Muslim whose family, at the time of Partition in 1947, came from India.
Mohba	An Indian tree.
Mujaheddin	Islamic guerrilla fighter, especially in the Middle East.
Mullah	Islam. A male religious teacher or leader
Namaste	A greeting or farewell gesture made by holding the palms together, as in prayer, and bowing the head.
Nan	Flat unleavened bread.

Nautch	A dance. A nautch girl is a dancing girl.
Nullah	A ravine or watercourse, normally dry in the dry season, caused by water erosion during floods.
Peshwa	The hereditary Mahratta ruler, similar to a Maharajah. Originally the Peshwas were the Chief Advisors, but they took over and became the Mahratta rulers.
Posteen	A sheepskin coat, at one time unique to Afghanistan.
Prasad	Food of the gods, comparable to communion wafers.
Puja	The act of worship or homage.
Puri	Mixed food fillings.
Rao	A title of honor, similar to a Rajah or a Rana.
Sahib	"Sir." Respectful title used to address someone (always male) in authority.
Samosa	A deep-fried triangular pastry filled with curried vegetables.
Serai	An inn, as in caravanserai. Normally very basic accommodation.
Shalimar	The decorative placement of lights in niches behind a waterfall to produce a shimmering curtain of falling water at night.
Shalwar kameez	A long blouse (shalwar) worn with trousers (kameez) by Muslim women.
Shamiana	A party tent, often decorated.
Shringara	Erotic temple carving.
Sweeper	A person who sweeps and cleans.

Tikis	Small snacks.
Tilak or Tika	The round red paste mark on the forehead that indicates you have worshipped that day. It can also be a caste mark.
Tempo	A motorized trishaw.
Tonga	A horse drawn cart.

Suggested Reading

My book is far removed from an academic work. For a collection of travel stories drawn from my notebooks I think it would be pretentious to offer a full bibliography. I list some of the books I've enjoyed and value. Some have been reprinted fairly recently, some are now rare, and many are out of print. Where I turn to history, my preferred sources are original journals. Clearly writing about Semiramis, the Assyrian warrior queen, we're getting obscure, and, I'd guess, into clay tablets. Chance led me to her. I was browsing in a secondhand book shop, and deep in the back shelves came across a three volume *History of British India*, published by Harper Brothers in New York in 1836. I found her there; and bought the books. But pause before you put in a search order for the set. Their thousand pages could put you off history forever. Its team of eight compilers, praiseworthy for their erudition and attention to detail, demand time and patience quite out of sync with our fast-track internet driven life today. Having acknowledged my source, I must confess my reportage on Semiramis and her problem solving takes a slightly different tone to theirs.

Afghanistan

Afghanistan has not been well favored by Western authors, simply because it has rarely been accessible, and welcoming, to foreign travelers. Anything written prior to the Soviet invasion in 1979 is dated, and the period between the Soviet withdrawal in 1988 and the Taliban clampdown in 1996 was was no window of opportunity for travel, for it was the time of Civil War. Patrick McCrory's *Signal Catastrophe* is out of print now. You could describe it as required reading for anyone contemplating the invasion, or the military occupation of Afghanistan.

James Michener's *Caravans* was last reprinted in paperback in 1982, and I was amazed to find it on a checkout bookstand in a supermarket in

Providenciales, Turks and Caicos Islands, in January 2003. The scope and sweep of this work of fiction opens on a compelling stage set. It is Afghanistan in 1946, when a mediaeval, splintered, tribal mountainous territory was attracting the interest of the United States, who were drawn into the area by the Realpolitik of the British abdication of the Indian sub-continent. Michener, in fact, did not visit Afghanistan until 1955, and *Caravans* was published in 1963. His stage set was ten years before his time, and twenty years before our time there.

What had changed by then? Kabul had gained a hotel (where we stayed), an airport, a paved road to the Russian border, which crossed the Hindu Kush through a tunnel (about which I write) at the Salang Pass, and some paved streets. All these facilities were used by the Soviets in their invasion of Afghanistan. The hotel became their headquarters.

The United States had paved the southern road from Kabul, through Kandahar, to Herat, initiated a dam project which gave electricity to Kandahar and irrigation to the Helmand valley. The irrigation of the desert was defeated by salinity. The US Government lost interest in Afghanistan, and the writing was on the wall. We all know the rest of the story.

McCrory, Patrick. *Signal Catastrophe, The Story of the Disastrous Retreat from Kabul* 1842. Hodder and Stouton, 1996.

Michener, James A. *Caravans*. Random House, 1963.

Pre-Mutiny India

I've not listed straightforward history books for the choice is wide, though many good ones are long out of print. For those interested in taking their history "on the rocks," as it were, *The New Cambridge History of India* is well worth attention, but it is lengthy. If you want to go back to the time of Clive, Mark Bence-Jones' book *Clive of India* is probably all you need to read. I find my most fascinating sources are the diaries of the women in the early days of British penetration into India. The 1830s was the best period. The accounts are refreshing for India is still a new excitement, an adventure almost beyond imagination, and the deadening influence of Victorian Britain, exported in tight-lipped bundles of disapproval, has yet to come about. So I take delight in Emily Eden and Miss Fane, and if you can find her book, read Janet Dunbar.

The New Cambridge History of India. I *The Mughals and their Contemporaries;* II *Indian States and the Transition to Colonialism;* III *The Indian Empire and the Beginnings of Modern Society;* IV *The Evolution of Contemporary South Asia.*

Bence-Jones, Mark. *Clive of India.* Constable & Company, 1974.

Eden, Emily. *Up the Country. Letters from India.* Curzon Press Ltd, 1978.

Miss Fane in India. John Pemble, Editor. Alan Sutton, 1985.

Dunbar, Janet. *Golden Interlude, The Edens in India 1836–1842.* John Murray, 1955.

The Indian Mutiny

In my Introduction I mentioned the extraordinary quantity of Indian Mutiny sources. If you want to see what I mean, get hold of Janice M. Ladendorf's annotated bibliography, *The Revolt in India 1857–58.* On the Rani of Jhansi my information came primarily from papers in the British India Office Library and Records and contemporary newspaper reports, backed by the thirty-plus titles on the Indian Mutiny of 1857-58 I have on my shelves. Each one, entirely colored by its political and national persuasion, offers a different slant.

If you want the best history of the period, there's no doubt that Kaye and Malleson's *History of the Indian Mutiny* in its six volumes is the one to choose. Moving to books of our time, Byron Farwell's *Queen Victoria's Little Wars* covers 1857 and the whole succession of petty wars that led to the establishment of the British Empire. For the revolt in shorter form than Kaye and Malleson, read Christopher Hibbert's *The Great Mutiny.*

There's not much material on the Indian side. *From Sepoy to Subedar,* Subedar Sita Ram's autobiography is interesting, particularly as it sets the scene in the pre-Mutiny Bengal Army. Surendra Nath Sen's *Eighteen Fifty-Seven* is a good modern history and well worth reading. I'd end my list in this section with a diary of the day and a novel. The diary is Mrs. Henry Duberly's *Campaigning Experiences in Rajpootana and Central India,* now long out of print, and the novel is John Master's *Nightrunners of Bengal.* If you want a book devoted to the Rani of Jhansi, your choices are very limited. D.V. Tahmankar's *The Ranee of Jhansi* is undoubtedly the best English language biography. Sir John Smythe (Brigadier The Rt Hon Sir John Smythe, Bt, VC, MC) wrote *The Rebellious Rani*, but it is jingoistic, heavily padded with British military history, and adds little to Tahmankar. Otherwise you must find your material in more general works, for the Rani of Jhansi hardly escapes attention. Perhaps the most modern work in which she features in part is Antonia Fraser's *The Warrior Queens.*

Ladendorf, Janice M. *The Revolt in India 1857–58*, Inter Documentation Company AG, 1966.

Kaye, Sir John, KCSI, FRS and Colonel Malleson CSI. *History of the Indian Mutiny of 1857-8.* W.H. Allen & Co Ltd, 1891.

Farwell, Byron. *Queen Victoria's Little Wars.* Norton, 1988.

Hibbert, Christopher. *The Great Mutiny India 1857.* Penguin Books, 1980.

Sita Ram, Sudebar. *From Sepoy to Subedar.* James Lunt, Editor. Papermac, 1970.

Nath Sen, Surendra. *Eighteen Fifty-Seven.* Government of India, 1957.

Duberly, Mrs Henry. *Campaigning Experiences in Rajpootana and Central India during the Suppression of the Mutiny 1857–1858.* Smith, Elder & Co., 1859.

Masters, John. *The Nightrunners of Bengal.* Michael Joseph, 1951.

Tahmankar, D.V. *The Ranee of Jhansi.* London: MacGibbon and Kee, 1958.

Smythe, Sir John. *The Rebellious Rani.* Frederick Muller, 1966.

Fraser, Antonia. *The Warrior Queens.* Alfred A. Knopf, 1989.

British India

I'll not dwell on this section for it's an easy field in which to find titles which attract. Jan Morris (James Morris in some titles), author of the *Pax Britannica Trilogy* is always worth reading, and her coffee table book, *The Spectacle of Empire*, is worth attention for its pictures. The India Office Library and Records have also published a book of photographs, *Victorian India in Focus*, which is brief but fascinating. Geoffrey Moorhouse's *India Britannica* is also strong on visual impact. These books apart, there is *Plain Tales From the Raj* and the very human Saumarez Smith letters titled, *A Young Man's Country*. Finally I'd say that Paul Scott's *Raj Quartet* is compulsory and compulsive reading to take you up to Indian Independence.

I was checking bookstores to see whether an edition of *Kim* could be found, other than in a series of Kipling's works, on the shelves today. I discovered to my surprise that there was a wide choice. The Norton Critical Edition of *Kim* was the most recent. If you find constant annotation an irritant and a distraction from the flow of the book, choose another version. Later you may want to use the Norton edition as a reference. If you can find a copy, Peter Hopkirk's *Quest for Kim, In Search of Kipling's Great Game*, is compelling reading in its own right; but you need to have read *Kim* first!

Morris, Jan. *The Spectacle of Empire. Style, Effect and the Pax Britannica*. Faber and Faber, 1982.

Desmond, Ray. *Victorian India in Focus*. Her Majesty's Stationery Office (for The India Office Library and Records), 1982.

Moorhouse, Geoffrey. *India Britannica*. William Collins & Co Ltd, 1983.

Plain Tales From the Raj. Images of British India in the twentieth century. Charles Allen, Editor. André Deutsch, 1975.

Smith, W.H. Saumarez. *A Young Man's Country. Letters of a Subdivisional Officer of the Indian Civil Service 1936–1937*. Michael Russell, 1977.

Scott, Paul. *The Raj Quartet*. *The Jewel in the Crown*. *The Day of the Scorpion*. *The Towers of Silence*. *A Division of the Spoils*. William Heinemann Ltd., 1966.

Kipling, Rudyard. *Kim* (The Norton Critical Edition). W. W. Norton and Company, 2002.

Hopkirk, Peter. *Quest for Kim, In Search of Kipling's Great Game*. Oxford University Press, 1977.

Kipling, Rudyard. *Kim*. MacMillan, 1901.

India After Independence

The lead-in to Independence, seen from the top, is well covered in Philip Ziegler's biography *Mountbatten* and there are many other books, not all of Mr Ziegler's persuasion, which deal with this period. I would not omit Jawaharlal Nehru's *The Discovery of India*, which was written during Nehru's period of internment in Ahmadnagar Fort Prison in 1944. It's a full book, and understandably dated in some respects; but it is, I think, vital reading. Paul Scott's sad little *Staying On* should be read, more so if you have enjoyed *The Raj Quartet*.

Ziegler, Philip. *Mountbatten*. William Collins & Co Ltd., 1985.

Nehru, Jawaharlal. *The Discovery of India*. Signet Press, 1948.

Scott, Paul. *Staying On*. William Heinemann Ltd., 1977.

Afghanistan, Pakistan, And India Today

Since the defeat of the Taliban in 2001-2002 the future state, security, and lifestyle of Afghanistan, and Pakistan and India has been at stake. Much has been written about the subcontinent since that date and hardly surprisingly many of the conclusions of one day have become invalid the next. At the time I write we are too close to history in the making to do more than take it day by day.

Illustration Key

Afghanistan. The basic simple mihrab arch in a mosque, which indicates the direction of Mecca, translated into an architectural gateway design.

Pakistan. A keel arch taken from the basic mihrab shape. Used to great effect, and the principal architectural feature, in the Taj Mahal.

India. A Hindu cusp arch, used by Akbar at Fatehpur Sikri. Evidence of his determination to blend the best of Hindu and Islamic architecture and arts, in a visible reinforcement of his ecumenism.

Dreams and Reality. A chattri. A domed cupola, a design feature taken into use both by Islamic and Hindu architects. Widely used in Northern India, particularly in the Golden Triangle and Rajasthan.

Drawing of a Bird in a Fruit Tree. Taken from inlaid marble decoration (pietra dura work) in the Taj Mahal.

Drawing of a War Elephant. War elephant armor on display in the Armoury in the Tower of London.